Sublime Soups

vegetarian soups and quick breads

Lenore Baum, M.A.
author of *Lenore's Natural Cuisine*

 Culinary Publications

Printed on acid-free paper

For inquiries, address:
Culinary Publications
Website www.lenoresnatural.com

Graphic designer: Shannon Terry
Cover art copyright © 2002 by Culinary Publications
Recipe icon illustrations copyright © 2002 by Don McLean

Library of Congress Control Number: 2002093123

ISBN 0-9674627-4-6

First Edition

table of contents

acknowledgments

First, I would like to express my warmest appreciation to my husband, Joe. He devoted countless hours helping me with the innumerable decisions involved in writing this book, as well as with the design, layout, editing and proofreading. Finally, Joe has also been my number one recipe taster through my experiments in natural foods cooking for the past thirteen years.

I am grateful to my teachers: Aveline Kushi, Cornelia Aihara, Wendy Esko, Diane Avoli, Marcia Halpern, Michio Kushi and Herman Aihara.

I also want to thank all of the superb cooks who unknowingly inspired me through their wonderful cookbooks: AnneMarie Colbin, Mary Estella, Margaret Lawson, Deborah Madison and Kristina Turner.

Specific thanks to Rachel Alpert Matez for *Double Baked Beans* and *Creamy Baked Anasazi Beans* which I adapted from her classic cookbook, *Cooking with Rachel*.

In appreciation to Jeff Woodward for *Cauliflower and Red Pepper Soup, Shiitake-Leek Miso Soup* and *Double Chickpea Soup* which I modified from his great cookbook, *The Healing Power of Food*.

I am particularly grateful to Meredith McCarty, author of *American Macrobiotic Cuisine, Fresh from a Vegetarian Kitchen* and *Sweet and Natural*. She motivated me to go beyond basic healing cooking to soul-satisfying, gourmet dishes. I also send my thanks to Meredith for her generosity in sharing her culinary wisdom with me and for allowing me to include some of her wonderful recipes in this cookbook: *Hot and Sour Soup, Almond Spread* and *Shiitake-Miso Soup with Garlic Toast*.

Lorna Sass is also due special appreciation. Thanks to Lorna, my recipes have evolved to include even more pressure-cooking. Beans dishes cooked in this one pot shorten cooking and clean-up time so dramatically, I find myself regularly making more gourmet recipes. Lorna has added spice to my life by introducing me to chile peppers. The amazingly sensual chipotle pepper, a smoked jalapeño, is an ingredient I now look forward to using with relish. Lastly, I highly recommend *Lorna's Curry Powder* over the store-bought variety. Her thoughtful blend of spices makes a huge contribution to the flavor of any curry dish.

I have modified Lorna's bean recipes by including kombu sea vegetable for added calcium and for its gas-fighting properties. I also reduced the amount of oil and made other minor changes. *Thai Vegetable Soup, Adzuki Chestnut Soup, Golden Autumn Soup, Dilled Broccoli Soup, Curried Split Pea Soup, Spicy Black Bean Chili* and *Express Chestnut Lentil Soup* were inspired or based on recipes from Lorna Sass' superb cookbooks, *Complete Vegetarian Kitchen* and *Cooking Under Pressure*.

Immeasurable appreciation to my extraordinary editors:

Anne Meuchel, my editor and creative consultant, for her collaboration and enthusiastic use of language. She transforms my pragmatic recipe names and stories to alluring and enticing descriptions. Anne organizes and polishes my writing with ease, while adding a dash of sparkle to every page she touches.

Ron Roush, for his boundless willingness to help, for his sense of design, skill at finding the perfect word, sage advice and great sense of humor. Ron has an uncommon skill for writing in everyday language and made sure that I kept culinary jargon accurate and to a minimum.

Sian Yardley, who persuaded me to begin editing my soup recipes just after *Lenore's Natural Cuisine* was published. Heartfelt appreciation for her continuing, meticulous efforts to make all of my recipes as clear and error-free as possible.

Jenelle Mazaris and Suzanne Gossett for proofreading, editing and insightful suggestions.

I am much obliged to the artists:

Joe Baum, for his concept and collaboration on the cover design.

Shannon Terry of Terry Koelzer Design, for her generous support of this project. I am especially grateful for her finesse of the page layout and persistent efforts to perfect the colors and balance on the cover. Shannon has a remarkably uncanny sense of what appeals to the eye.

Heartfelt gratitude is due to my dedicated cooking school assistants who have generously supported my work: Rachel Thornberry, Patty Schniers, Gloria Mathiesen, Debra Walter, Francine Harper, Anne Meuchel, Jenelle Mazaris, Chris Popa, Nora Wojciechowski, Suzanne Gossett and Angela Allen.

Lastly, I would like to thank my students and friends for their steadfast support.

introduction

Historically, out of necessity, cooks poured whatever ingredients were available into a pot of boiling water to create a meal for the family. Soup was born. It is my favorite food to cook any time of year. It is warming, nourishing and satisfying as well as wholesome, simple and convenient. Hot soup stimulates the appetite and relaxes the digestive system. It also fills up a menu quickly. Soup can be an impromptu meal, snack, travel food or can even be used as a sauce over rice or noodles.

About 25 years ago, while I was living in Arizona, I started my serious ventures in vegetarian cooking by experimenting with soup. My friends enjoyed my creations and began asking me to sell them. My cooking career began with my small deli, Lenore's Soups du Jour. Later, I attended the Kushi Institute and Vega Study Center to expand my skills and to learn the principles of healing cooking. While I enjoyed learning more about healthful main dishes and desserts, soups remained my number one passion.

Homemade soup is so much more nutritious than soup from a can or from a restaurant, which is usually laden with sodium and fat. Soup is also one of the most forgiving foods to cook. By that, I mean that just about any recipe can be successful with relative ease. If the consistency of your soup is too thick or too runny, you can easily thin or thicken it. You can also boost its flavor after cooking with a quick dash of shoyu or umeboshi vinegar. Finally, homemade soups and stews make great leftovers. They often taste even better the next day, after the flavors have had time to marry.

I like to pair homemade quick breads with my soups. Muffins can be made in less time than it takes to make a pot of soup. So, there is no reason to resort to inferior, store-bought ones. The nutritious breads in this book are cholesterol-free, lactose-free and most of all, delicious. Since quick breads freeze well, they are handy to keep around for a last-minute accompaniment to soup and salad.

After many years of cooking and teaching classes, I knew it was time to gather my favorite recipes in one place. Thus, *Sublime Soups* was born. These days, I make a steaming pot of soup every week. It is waiting then, ready to warm, soothe and nourish.

soup and stew basics

helpful hints

following a recipe

Before beginning to cook, it is important to read through the entire recipe and any cook's tips. Next, prepare and measure all of the ingredients. I like to use stainless steel bowls to hold cut vegetables and measured herbs or spices until it's time to use them. If you follow this method, you will not find yourself scrambling for ingredients at the last minute.

unfamiliar foods and utensils

Unfamiliar foods are explained in the Glossary. You can leave out or substitute ingredients if you do not have them on hand, however, I feel that certain ingredients are worth the extra effort. For example, kombu can be omitted, but its health benefits justify a trip to the natural food store.

Unfamiliar utensils are described in "Essential Tools and Equipment." Most tools are available in stores that sell kitchen tools. However, if you have difficulty finding an item, refer to the Mail Order Sources in the Appendix.

chiles

Chiles used in these recipes are fresh unless noted otherwise. To handle fresh, hot chile peppers, I recommend that you set aside a pair of latex gloves just for this purpose. The seeds and inner membrane are the hottest parts of the pepper. Simply washing your hands does not remove the volatile chile oils that will burn your eyes or mouth if touched. Although delicious, hot chile peppers are not recommended on a healing diet. Simply omit them from my recipes and adjust the flavor to your taste.

abbreviations

TBS. = Tablespoon
1/2 TBS. = 1 1/2 teaspoons
tsp. = teaspoon

cutting methods

When the recipe calls for vegetables to be blended, cut them into large pieces to save preparation time.

Cut each vegetable into pieces of the same size for even cooking. For variety, choose different cutting techniques, see page 161. For stews and peasant soups, vegetables can be cut into large pieces.

cooking time

These recipes have been tested at sea level. Cooking times may vary. At higher elevations, cooking times should be increased and might take some experimentation. If this is a concern, contact the food editor of your local newspaper for advice.

Check for doneness close to the recommended cooking time. Insert the point of a sharp paring knife into vegetables to test for tenderness. For beans, it is best to taste them.

cooking terms

boiling
To cook over high heat until bubbles appear, or as my mother says, "until the water dances."

dry-roasting
To toast ingredients in a hot skillet, without oil, until golden brown in color.

pressure-cooking
To cook in a sealed pot under about fifteen pounds of pressure per square inch. My recipes will indicate whether to quick-release or natural-release the pressure-cooker when the cooking time is over.

> **quick-release:** place the pressure-cooker in the sink with the lid locked in place. Run cold water over the pressure-cooker until the pressure valve comes down. Then, you can safely open the lid.

> **natural-release**: remove the pressure cooker from the heat source and allow the pressure to come down on its own. For more information about pressure-cooking or alternatives to pressure-cooking, see "Essential Tools and Equipment," page 13.

sautéing
To cook food quickly in a small amount of oil. Test whether the pan is hot enough by sprinkling several drops of water in it. When the water sizzles, add the oil, but do not heat it to the smoking point. I often recommend sautéing vegetables before adding them to the soup pot. This adds flavor and depth. However, you can eliminate this step and the oil. This makes for faster preparation, although some flavor will be lost.

simmering

To cook gently over low heat, just below the boiling point. Bubbles will occasionally break the surface. When simmering beans, I keep the pot lid ajar to prevent spillovers and stir occasionally. To simmer beans rather than pressure-cook them, adjust the cooking time on my recipes by referring to the Bean Cooking Chart on page 162.

steaming

To cook in a covered pot, in which a steamer basket is placed above the boiling water. When frozen or refrigerated muffins are steamed, they become aromatic and taste as if they have just come from the oven.

general guidelines

Be flexible. If you're out of a particular vegetable or bean, substitute a different one. Or, simply omit it. Add more or less garlic, onions, salt, shoyu or miso to your own taste.

Some soups thicken as they stand. You can add water to thin them and adjust the flavor before serving by adding shoyu to taste. Or, if a soup is too thin, you can thicken it using the following method: whisk one teaspoon of kudzu or 2 teaspoons of cornstarch or arrowroot in 1/4 cup of cool water. Add it to the hot soup, return to a simmer and stir until it thickens, about 3 minutes.

Soup is one of the few leftovers that improves with time. It is even more delicious the next day after the flavors have had time to marry. I recommend making large quantities. You can eat it for breakfast, lunch, dinner or as a healthy snack. You can even blend it to use as a sauce over rice or noodles. Soup is also a good choice for casual entertaining and unexpected guests. Finally, it can easily be transported anywhere in a thermos.

serving and storing

serving

The soup serving size, noted on each recipe, is an eight-ounce portion and is usually served as part of a meal. When the main meal is centered around soup, serve 12- to 16-ounce portions.

Please remember that presentation is important. Most of us eat with our eyes as well as our mouths. It adds a lot to soups and stews to garnish them with something raw and green. Consider minced scallions, parsley, cilantro or other fresh herbs. This adds bright splashes of color, flavor and the dynamic element of cooked versus raw.

storing prepared food

Homemade soups, stews, quick breads and spreads will keep refrigerated for about a week, unless otherwise noted. Of course, the fresher the food, the more vital and nutritious it is. Realistically, though, it is healthier to eat leftover, homemade soup than soup from a can.

I strongly believe in storing food in glass jars. Glass, unlike plastic, is an inert material, which is non-reactive with food. A bonus is that you can see what is inside. I prefer wide-mouth canning jars. I have even dedicated an entire shelf to them in my kitchen! A stainless steel canning funnel (see Mail Order Sources) makes filling them a breeze. When freezing soup in a glass jar, allow two inches of "head" space at the top for expansion to prevent breakage.

essential ingredients

water

Most of us know that it's important to drink eight to ten glasses of water a day. This is solid advice, especially if the water is purified. According to Dr. Andrew Weil, recent data reveals that over one million Americans drink water that contains significant levels of cancer-causing chemicals: arsenic, radon and chlorine by-products. He recommends a reverse osmosis or carbon-KDF system (see Mail Order Sources) to purify water. Since impurities from plumbing and hot water tanks can leach into the water, it is equally important not to use hot, tap water for cooking, washing or soaking food. Lastly, research has reported that chemicals in plastic bottles can leach into the water inside. In conclusion, it's far better to use your own freshly-filtered water.

stock

Although many cookbook authors recommend making a stock with vegetables, beef or chicken for the soup base, I have not found that the extra time and effort is necessary. Bean soups have plenty of flavor, texture and body on their own. To boost the flavor of simple vegetable soups, I use miso and occasionally use organic, dried herb seasonings, such as Herbamere®. Add one-half teaspoon of Herbamere® per quart of water to make an instant vegetable broth. However, be aware that most seasoning blends contain salt, so adjust your own recipes accordingly.

thickeners

I prefer kudzu because it is a natural thickener, although you can substitute cornstarch or arrowroot. Use twice what the recipe calls for when substituting either of these thickeners.

onions

The common yellow onion is used in these recipes.

sea salt

Good quality sea salt, in moderation, is necessary for digestion, nerve connections and muscle contractions. It assists the immune system by inhibiting the growth of harmful bacteria, viruses, fungi, parasites and by enhancing proper intestinal flora. Recommended high quality sources of salt include unrefined sea salt, miso and shoyu. You can substitute 1 teaspoon of sea salt for approximately 2 tablespoons of miso or shoyu.

miso

Miso is an aged, fermented soybean paste made from cooked soybeans and salt. The two main types of miso are dark and light. Dark commonly refers to barley miso, which has been aged for at least two years. It has a salty taste and is used in dark-colored soups, gravies and stews. Light miso has a sweeter taste because it contains less salt and is fermented for less time. It is used in light-colored soups and sauces. Regardless of the type, unpasteurized miso contains friendly bacteria, high quality protein and digestive enzymes. Since digestive enzymes are destroyed by high heat, it is best not to boil soup after adding miso to it. I frequently use miso to provide a depth of flavor, normally achieved through making time-consuming stock. Superior, Japanese miso as well as high-quality American-made South River Miso® and Miso Master® are available in well-stocked natural food stores and through mail order

kombu

I always use this dried, mineral-rich sea vegetable in bean recipes. It helps prevent gastric distress and adds calcium, other trace minerals and flavor!

fats

Fats lend a satisfying mouth-feel and taste to food. Monounsaturated fats are considered the healthiest choice. They are found in vegetable and seed oils like canola, olive and sesame oil. In place of butter or margarine, I use Spectrum Naturals® Canola Spread. It's non-hydrogenated and tastes like butter. You can ask the server to bring olive oil with the bread basket at most restaurants. It's best to avoid saturated fats, found mostly in coconut and palm kernel oils, animal fats and dairy products. Research has linked these fats to heart disease, cancer and other serious illnesses.

organic

Organic foods are those grown without the use of chemical fertilizers and pesticides. Pesticides are poisons designed to kill living organisms, such as bacteria and mold, and have been linked to cancer in humans. Recent studies show that random samples of vegetables from supermarkets can contain high levels of pesticides. Ironically, it is a good thing to find bug holes and other imperfections in organic produce. This indicates that the produce was not sprayed with pesticides!

Although organic foods are generally higher in cost, you may find your good health is well worth the expense. Buying organic also supports small farmers who care about the quality of the soil and the environment. Shop at your local farmers' market and encourage farmers to grow vegetables without pesticides. After hearing customers ask for pesticide-free produce, they may take action.

Finally, the natural flavor of vegetables is masked by the bitter flavor of pesticides. Because of this, organic vegetables taste sweeter than their sprayed counterparts. This is especially noticeable with carrots.

naturally-leavened bread

Conventionally-yeasted breads have been linked to health problems. Naturally-leavened breads, such as real sourdough, are a more wholesome complement to soups and stews.

Unfortunately, many so-called healthful whole wheat loaves, pita breads and crackers are yeasted. If you do not have a natural sourdough baker in your area, you can bake this kind of bread yourself. For recipes, see Meredith McCarty's cookbook, *Fresh From A Vegetarian Kitchen*. Alternatively, you can ask your local natural food store to stock French Meadows® sourdough breads. Whole Foods Market® is a national chain of natural food stores that sells several varieties of naturally-leavened breads.

essential tools and equipment

You have undoubtedly already discovered that well-chosen kitchen tools and equipment make cooking easier and more enjoyable. Every cook should own at least one high quality knife and several nonstick pans. If you invest in some of these tools, you will reap enormous timesavings. Visit our website, www.lenoresnatural.com for hard-to-find items.

It's no secret that nonstick pots and pans make cooking and clean up a breeze. However, I do not recommend pots with chemical coatings like Teflon® and Silverstone®, which are believed to be carcinogenic and eventually flake off into the food. I use Scanpan® nonstick, ceramic titanium-coated pots and skillets, which are virtually indestructible. They allow low-fat cooking without scorching and without the risk of chemicals getting into the food.

blender: the best appliance for creating an ultra-smooth consistency. Adding the soup in batches, one cup at a time prevents spillovers. Also, a damp dishcloth held over the top of a closed blender prevents the hot mixture from splashing out. Choose a model with about 300 watts of power. You need only high and low settings and a pulse feature to make great soups.

Dutch oven: a 5- or 6-quart pot with a heavy bottom to retain heat. This pot saves clean up by doing double duty. It's perfect for first sautéing soup ingredients, then for simmering the soup. You can also use it as a baked bean pot that can go directly into the oven. If you do not have a Dutch oven, you can use a flame tamer under a heavy or nonstick pot.

flame tamer: also known as a heat diffuser. This tool diffuses the direct heat of the stovetop, preventing beans and grains from burning or scorching. The flame tamer can be used on both gas and electric stove tops and is available in well-stocked houseware and hardware stores. Preheat the flame tamer several minutes on another burner before placing it under a simmering pot.

immersion blender: a wand-like electric tool with small blades. It is inserted directly into the cooking pot to purée food, reducing preparation and clean-up time. It works best with vegetable soups. It does not, however, shred the outer skin of beans smoothly enough for bean soups.

knives: the most important tools in the kitchen! I like to use superior, razor-sharp knives: a Japanese, square-end knife for cutting vegetables and a drop-forged 8-inch chef's knife for cutting dense winter squash. A paring knife is also useful.

miscellaneous: a timer, measuring spoons, measuring cups, vegetable peeler, tongs, whisk and a slotted spoon.

miso strainer: ideal for puréing miso directly in the soup pot. Otherwise, you must place a small amount of the hot soup in a small bowl, add the miso, whisk until smooth and return it to the pot.

pot cleaning tips:

I use the superior aluminum and stainless steel cleaner, Cameo®, to scrub off the thin residue from the inside of stainless steel pots.

In a burned pot, dissolve 3 tablespoons of granulated, dishwasher detergent dissolved in 3 cups of hot water. Boil, covered for 20 minutes. Wash thoroughly with soap.

pressure cooker: a sealed pot that cooks food under fifteen pounds of pressure. Pressure-cooking quickly tenderizes food, reducing cooking time by up to 80%. A bean soup that requires two hours to cook in a stock pot can be pressure-cooked in 12 minutes! Best of all, pressure-cookers create mouth-watering dishes because the flavors marry in the pot. The new, second generation pressure cookers are completely safe to use. For more information, see Lorna Sass' *Great Vegetarian Cooking Under Pressure.*

Do not fill a pressure cooker more than half full when cooking beans. If it is filled higher than this, the loose outer shells of the beans can clog the pressure valve. For information on releasing the pressure, see page 8.

skimmer: a fine mesh, stainless steel tool used to skim off foam that rises to the surface when boiling beans.

stock pot: a 6- or 8-quart stainless steel pot used for making large quantities of soup.

tea ball: a mesh ball used for loose tea infusion. I put bay leaves in a tea ball during cooking. This helps to recover and discard them before blending. Alternatively, you can place bay leaves in a piece of cheesecloth tied with string.

visit: www.lenoresnatural.com for hard-to-find items.

all about beans

B eans, lentils, peanuts and split peas are known as legumes since their seeds grow in pods. Generally, they are all referred to as beans. By whatever name, they are hearty, nourishing and versatile. I use them frequently to make rich, luscious soups and dips.

Beans are inexpensive, yet packed with nutrients and health benefits. A mere half-cup of cooked beans provides 25% of the daily requirement of fiber, 30% of folic acid, 15% of iron and 7 grams of protein. In fact, beans offer twice as much protein as grains. Moreover, this same half-cup of beans can lower cholesterol and blood pressure, control blood sugar levels and maintain healthy intestines. In conclusion, beans are the most nutritious, healing and satisfying alternative to meat!

With all of these good qualities, you would think that everyone would be bean crazy. Yet, there is one drawback that no one wants to mention in polite company - flatulence. Why does this happen? Beans contain indigestible complex sugars, oliogosaccharides, which feed harmless intestinal bacteria. Before long, fermentation takes place and the bacteria emit gas, causing us to do the same! Luckily, there are many remedies for this problem. Since none is a cure-all, try them alone or in combination to see which works for you.

remedies for gastric distress

Soaking beans overnight will eliminate up to 75% of the indigestible oliogosaccharides.

Use a skimmer or slotted spoon to remove foam, the indigestible oliogosaccharides, from the surface of soup until the foam subsides. This step usually takes about fifteen minutes. If you're in a hurry, five minutes will do.

Add kombu sea vegetable, which not only makes beans softer and more digestible, but adds calcium and other essential minerals to the bean dish.

Take a digestive enzyme with the first bite, such as Yes to Beans® or Beano®. Yes to Beans® works best for me.

Add aromatic herbs and spices, such as bay leaves, ginger, cumin and curry to the bean pot.

Begin by eating small portions of beans or bean soups several times a week to acclimate your digestive system to them.

For a particularly delicate digestive tract:

> Eat beans only with vegetables. Avoid combining beans with fruits or grains.

> After soaking, boil the beans 5 minutes and discard the water. Repeat two more times before proceeding with the recommended cooking method.

preparation

For the freshest beans, purchase them from a store with a high turnover. Beans, stored too long, dry out and remain tough during cooking. They are best used within six months. With older, stored beans, try increasing the cooking time.

Before cooking beans, pick them over to remove small pebbles, debris, clumps of dirt and broken beans. To wash beans, place them in a bowl, cover with water and rub the beans between your hands. Rinse them until the rinse water is clear. You can pour the rinse water over a white plate to make this easier to see.

Soaking beans makes them more digestible and allows them to cook more quickly. Soak them in a large bowl, since they will double in size. After soaking, place the beans in a colander and rinse them thoroughly.

> **overnight soak:** cover with water, two inches above the level of dried beans. Let stand overnight.

> **speedy soak:** place the beans in a pot. Cover with water two inches above the level of the dried beans. Bring the pot to a boil, then turn off the heat and let stand, covered, for one hour.

cooking

Do not fill the pressure cooker more than half full when cooking beans to prevent the pressure valve from clogging.

To prevent the beans from boiling over while cooking in a stock pot, keep the lid ajar.

Add salt, miso, shoyu and vinegar at the end of cooking time. If added sooner, these ingredients will not allow the outer skin of the beans to soften. When cooking beans in a pressure cooker, add these ingredients after the pressure has been released.

Bean soups thicken as they stand. Before serving, thin slightly with water and adjust the salty flavor with miso, shoyu or salt.

If soup is too thin, you can easily thicken it by puréing it in a blender. Or, whisk one teaspoon of kudzu in 1⁄4 cup of water. Then, add it to the hot soup, simmer and stir until this mixture becomes translucent, about 3 minutes.

Many recipes are pressure-cooked to save time. You can use a stock pot instead. Refer to the Bean Cooking Chart, page 162, to adjust the cooking time.

storage

Store dried beans and grains in a cool place in non-plastic containers like glass jars or paper bags. Plastic containers will eventually impart a chemical taste these foods.

Freeze leftover, cooked bean dishes in small portions so they can be a quick addition to a meal.

Freeze leftover bean soups in glass jars. Remember to leave two inches of space at the top of the jar.

all about vegetables

Be sure to thoroughly wash vegetables before using them. If organic, simply scrub off the surface dirt with a natural brush just before cooking. However, if time is a constraint, it is better to wash them early in the day rather than use frozen vegetables.

When organic produce is unavailable, you can remove pesticides from the surface of produce. Add a few drops of a mild, coconut-based soap, such as Shaklee® Basic H® to a sink filled with about three inches of water. Clean the produce in this soapy solution and rinse well. Although this emulsifies oily pesticides from the surface of produce, most pesticides are absorbed during the growth cycle and cannot be removed from the inside of fruits and vegetables.

Be aware that commercial rutabagas and bell peppers are usually waxed to extend their shelf life. You must peel rutabagas or other heavily-waxed vegetables since washing will not remove this coating.

helpful hints

Store vegetables in the refrigerator in tightly closed plastic bags. Evert-Fresh Bag®, an excellent reusable storage bag, doubles the shelf life of stored produce.

Instead of holding yams, onions, garlic and winter squash in the refrigerator, store them in a cool, well-ventilated area like a basement.

Save time and include highly beneficial fiber in your diet by not peeling vegetables. There are several exceptions: tough outer skin found on broccoli stalks and butternut squash, or waxed skin found on commercial rutabagas.

Cut each vegetable into pieces of the same size for even cooking. For variety, choose different cutting techniques, see page 161.

Vegetables cut into larger pieces are more suitable for stews, which are cooked longer over low heat. This cutting style also works well for rustic, peasant soups.

To quickly dice onions, place 2-inch pieces of onion, one level deep, in a food processor, fitted with a metal blade. Briefly pulse. Remove the diced onions and repeat with more onions. Do not use this method when sautéing, however, as too much water will be released. If you plan to sauté onions, it is best to cut them with a knife.

When sautéing vegetables before adding them to the soup pot, heat the oil just to the sizzling point. This occurs when a few drops of water sprinkled in the hot pan begin to sizzle. Do not allow oil to reach the smoking point, because this creates free radicals. Scientists believe that these compounds cause many modern-day ailments, as well as premature aging.

It is best not to sauté garlic in oil for more than one minute, or it will become bitter. Also, you can increase the anti-carcinogenic benefits of garlic if you cut it and allow it to stand for 10 minutes before cooking it.

When soups are to be blended, cut the vegetables into large pieces to reduce preparation time.

notes

vegetable soups

Y ou can easily include the daily vegetable requirement into your family's diet by making vegetable soups. They will nourish your body, mind and waistline, too. Low in fat, you can freely indulge in an abundance of luscious vegetables. Since they are packed with fiber, they even give you a full feeling without the calories!

I particularly like to include sweet vegetables like carrots, winter squash, onions and parsnips in my soups. They satisfy the sweet tooth, maintain blood sugar levels and nourish the middle organs: the liver, spleen and pancreas. Traditional medicine believes that by nourishing these organs, the body becomes relaxed, reducing stress and worry. *Golden Squash Soup*, *Sweet Buttercup Soup* and *Sweet Miso Soup* are several recipes that feature these vegetables.

Many Americans are accustomed to eating something sweet for breakfast, such as sugary cereals or doughnuts. For a more healthful choice, try eating any of the following sweet *and* nourishing soups with a muffin of your choice:

See "All About Vegetables" for helpful information about their preparation, page 18.

sweet miso soup

12 servings

Soup for breakfast! It sounds crazy, but once you try it, you may be hooked. Warm and nourishing, it gives you a better jump-start than any cup of java, without the caffeine. Serve it with a toasted English muffin or sourdough bread with Savory Bagel Spread, page 127.

ingredients

8 cups water
1 6-inch strip wakame
1 small buttercup squash
1 medium onion, cut into thin
  1/2 rounds

1 small daikon radish, cut into
  thin 1/2 rounds
6 TBS. barley miso or to taste
1 scallion, thinly sliced, to garnish,
  optional

directions

1. Bring 8 cups of water to a boil in a large stock pot.

2. **Meanwhile,** cover the wakame with water and let soak for 5 minutes. Cut it into 1/2-inch squares and set aside.

3. Remove the blemished areas from the squash skin. Leave the remaining skin intact. Cut in half lengthwise, from top to bottom and scoop out the seeds. Trim away the stem and blossom ends. Cut into 1/2-inch cubes and set aside.

4. Add the onion and wakame to the pot. Simmer uncovered 5 minutes. Add the daikon and simmer until fork-tender, about 5 minutes.

5. Add the squash and simmer uncovered until fork-tender, about 5 minutes. Remove from the heat.

6. Place a small amount of the hot soup in a small bowl, add the miso, whisk until smooth and return it to the pot. Stir and serve garnished with scallion.

variations

- Substitute carrots, rutabaga, parsnips, cabbage or butternut squash for the buttercup squash.
- Add 1 cup of diced daikon greens or other greens to step #5.
- Add 2 slices of fresh ginger to step #6.

cook's tips

- To make a one-pot breakfast meal, add leftover cooked rice, millet or noodles to the soup just before serving.
- Use an 8-inch chef's knife to cut through the dense skin of buttercup squash. Hold the squash securely on a cutting board, stem side up. Place the tip of the knife into the top of the squash, next to the stem, and cut with a rocking downward motion. Repeat on the other side.
- To preserve the friendly bacteria and enzymes in miso soup, do not boil it when reheating. For the same reason, do not freeze it. Since it will keep refrigerated, I make a batch large enough to provide a bowl of miso soup every morning for a week.

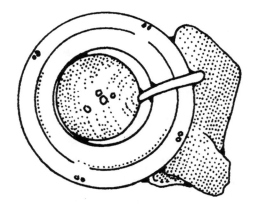

shiitake-miso soup with garlic toast

4 servings

This soup is a perfect opener for a big dinner. Its light broth will relax the digestive tract for the meal ahead, without filling you up. Garlic Toast *garnish adds a lively touch.*

ingredients

4 dried shiitake mushrooms
4 cups water
1 3-inch strip wakame
4 cups water
1 TBS. kudzu, dissolved in 1/4 cup cool water

1/4 cup sweet, white miso
1 TBS. fresh lemon juice
2 TBS. scallion, thinly sliced, to garnish
4 slices *Garlic Toast,* page 143

directions

1. Rinse the shiitake mushrooms. Place them in a bowl and add boiling water to cover. Soak for 20 minutes, placing a plate over the bowl to hold in the heat. Place the wakame in another bowl and cover with water. Soak for 5 minutes. Cut it into 1-inch squares and set aside.

2. **Meanwhile,** bring 4 cups of water to a boil in a medium pot. Add the wakame.

3. Cut off the mushroom stems and discard. Cut the caps into 1/4-inch strips and add them to the pot. Cover and simmer until tender, about 20 minutes.

4. **Meanwhile,** prepare the *Garlic Toast.*

5. Add the dissolved kudzu to the pot and stir until the soup thickens, about 3 minutes.

6. Place a small amount of the hot soup in a small bowl, add the miso, whisk until smooth and return it to the pot. Add the lemon juice, stir and serve garnished with *Garlic Toast* and scallions.

minestrone soup

12 servings

Chock-full of sweet vegetables, this variation of a classic nourishes you with butternut squash, carrots, onions and parsnips. According to traditional Asian medicine, sweet vegetables also reduce anxiety.

ingredients

4 cups water
3⁄4 pound butternut squash, diced
1⁄2 parsnip, sliced
1 large carrot, sliced
1 garlic clove, minced
1 small onion, 1⁄2 rounds
1⁄8 head cabbage, shredded
1 tsp. unrefined sea salt
4 ounces corn macaroni
3⁄4 pound green beans, diced
1⁄2 tsp. shoyu

4 cups *Untomato Sauce*, page 147
   or tomato sauce
3⁄4 pound broccoli, separated into
   florets, peeled stalks, cut into thin
   slices
2 stalks celery, sliced
1⁄8 tsp. dried basil
1⁄8 tsp. dried marjoram
1⁄8 tsp. dried thyme
1⁄8 tsp. dried dill
2 TBS. scallions, thinly sliced, to
   garnish

directions

1. Bring 4 cups of water to a boil in a 4-quart pot. Add the squash, parsnip, carrot, garlic, onion, cabbage and salt. Simmer for 5 minutes.

2. **Meanwhile,** cook the corn macaroni al dente, 8 - 10 minutes. Pour through a colander and rinse until cool. Set aside.

3. Add the green beans, shoyu and *Untomato Sauce* to the soup pot. Simmer for 5 minutes.

4. Add the broccoli, celery and herbs. Simmer for 3 minutes.

5. Add the macaroni and serve garnished with scallions.

variations

- Cut the vegetables into whatever size or shape you prefer.
- Blend 1 quart of the soup and mix with the remaining quart for a creamier consistency.
- Omit the *Untomato Sauce* or the organic tomato sauce. This recipe will then make 8 servings.
- Substitute a different type of pasta for the corn macaroni.
- Rinse, then add one 15-ounce can of kidney beans to step #4.

sweet buttercup soup

6 servings

For a light appetizer, try this no-fuss vegetable soup. Its simple sweetness also makes it a favorite of children.

ingredients

1 onion, diced medium
1 medium buttercup squash, unpeeled, bite-size pieces
1/2 tsp. dried, ground oregano

2 TBS. chickpea miso
2 TBS. fresh parsley, minced, to garnish

directions

1. Add the onion to a 4-quart pot. Barely cover with water. Simmer uncovered for 20 minutes.

2. Add the squash and oregano. Cover and simmer until the squash is tender, about 15 minutes.

3. Place a small amount of the hot soup in a small bowl, add the miso, whisk until smooth and return it to the pot. Stir and serve garnished with parsley.

cook's tip

- Scrub the squash and trim away any brown spots on the skin. Cut the squash in half, top to bottom. Scoop out the seeds, trim away stem at top and bottom. Cut into 1/2-inch cubes.

cauliflower and red pepper soup

8 servings

Cauliflower lovers - this soup is for you! The contrasting colors of red and white make a lovely presentation. Serve with Homemade Sesame-Rice Crackers, *page 142, to complete this light, Asian meal.*

ingredients

1 small red bell pepper, diced small
1/2 tsp. sesame oil
1 onion, cut into large pieces
5-6 cups cauliflower, cut into large pieces

3 cups boiling water
1/4 cup sweet, white miso
1 scallion, thinly sliced, to garnish

directions

1. Preheat the oven to 350°. Place the diced red pepper on a baking sheet. Bake for 25 - 30 minutes, then set aside.

2. **Meanwhile,** heat the oil in a nonstick Dutch oven. Sauté the onion until translucent, about 5 minutes. Move the onion to one side of the pot and add a few more drops of oil to the cleared space. Add the cauliflower and sauté for 3 - 4 minutes.

3. Add 3 cups of boiling water to the pot. Cover and simmer until the cauliflower is soft, about 10 minutes.

4. Transfer the soup to a blender. Process until a smooth consistency is reached, adding more water as needed. Return the purée to the pot and simmer for 3 minutes. Serve garnished with the baked red bell pepper and scallions.

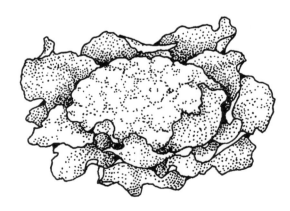

shiitake-leek miso soup

6 servings

Dried shiitake mushrooms add an earthy flavor and color contrast to green leeks. They are reputed by traditional medicine to help dissolve fat and cysts.

ingredients

6 dried shiitake mushrooms

1 6-inch strip wakame

1/4 tsp. sesame oil

1 cup leeks, cut into 1-inch matchsticks

2 cups green cabbage, shredded

5 cups boiling water

3 TBS. brown rice miso

directions

1. Rinse the shiitake mushrooms. Place them in a bowl and add boiling water to cover. Soak for 20 minutes, placing a plate over the bowl to hold in the heat. Place the wakame in another bowl and cover with water. Soak for 5 minutes. Cut it into 1-inch squares and set aside.

2. Cut off the mushroom stems and discard. Cut the caps into thin strips.

3. Heat the oil in a 4-quart pot. Sauté the leeks and mushrooms for 5 minutes. Add the cabbage to the pot and sauté for 5 minutes.

4. Add the wakame and 5 cups of boiling water to the pot. Cover and simmer for 30 minutes.

5. **Meanwhile,** place a small amount of the hot soup in a small bowl, add the miso, whisk until smooth and return it to the pot.

variations

* Substitute barley miso for brown rice miso.
* For added flavor, add 1/2 teaspoon of Herbamere® seasoning to step #5.

broccoli squash purée

10 servings

One day, it took forever to retrieve some bay leaves from a large pot of soup. I was determined to find an easier way. Placing the bay leaf inside a mesh tea ball was my joyful discovery. It even has a chain and hook so it can hang nicely from the edge of the pot! Try this technique when making this recipe. Serve with Herbal Corn Muffins, *page 133.*

ingredients

1 cup small broccoli florets, to garnish
1/2 tsp. extra-virgin olive oil
1 medium onion, coarsely cut
3 medium garlic cloves, cut in half
3 cups broccoli stalks, peeled and coarsely cut
2 cups yellow summer squash, coarsely cut

1 tsp. unrefined sea salt
3 cups boiling water
1 bay leaf, in a tea ball
1/2 tsp. dried basil
1/2 tsp. dried marjoram
1/2 tsp. dried thyme
2 pinches white pepper, optional
1 cup EdenBlend® beverage

directions

1. Steam the broccoli florets until fork-tender, about 2 minutes. Reserve for the garnish.

2. Heat the oil in a nonstick Dutch oven. Sauté the onion until translucent, about 5 minutes. Add the garlic, stirring constantly for 1 minute.

3. Add the broccoli stalks and remaining ingredients, except the EdenBlend® beverage. Cover and simmer until the vegetables are tender, about 10 minutes.

4. Discard the bay leaf. Blend the soup in batches until smooth. Stir in the EdenBlend® beverage and simmer for 3 minutes. Serve garnished with the steamed broccoli florets.

variation
• Substitute sesame oil for the olive oil.

cook's tips
• Black pepper is reputed to irritate the intestines. I prefer milder, white pepper.
• For added flavor, use Herbamere®, an organic herb seasoning salt. Add 1/2 teaspoon for every 4 cups of water.
• Use an immersion blender to reduce clean up.

delicate vegetable soup

4 servings

When I find myself craving vegetables, I reach for this recipe. Herbamere®, an organic herb seasoning, builds flavor fast. It is good any time of day.

ingredients

1/2 tsp. extra-virgin olive oil
1 medium onion, coarsely chopped
1 garlic clove, cut in half
1/2 tsp. dried thyme
1/2 tsp. dried basil
1/2 tsp. Herbamere®

2 pinches cayenne pepper
3 cups boiling water
1/2 cup rolled oats
3 cups broccoli, separated into florets and peeled stalks cut into large pieces

directions

1. Heat the oil in a nonstick Dutch oven or soup pot. Sauté the onion until translucent, about 5 minutes. Add the garlic and sauté, stirring constantly for 1 minute.

2. **Meanwhile,** steam 1 cup of small broccoli florets until al dente, about 2 minutes. Set aside for the garnish.

3. Add the remaining broccoli florets and stalks, thyme, basil, Herbamere®, cayenne, boiling water and rolled oats. Cover and simmer for 15 minutes.

4. Transfer the soup to a blender and process until thick and creamy. Add more Herbamere® to taste. Serve garnished with broccoli florets.

variation

*   Add cayenne pepper to taste in step #4.

french onion soup with baked croutons

12 servings

This version of a classic French soup eliminates the beef, but not the time-honored flavor. The secret is the caramelized onions. Mirin, a natural rice wine, adds an undertone of sweetness. Top with Baked Croutons.

ingredients

1 tsp. canola oil
5 onions, thin 1/2 rounds
1 6-inch strip kombu, soaked and
   thinly sliced
1 pinch of sage
1 pinch of thyme

5 cups boiling water
1/2 tsp. unrefined sea salt
1/4 cup shoyu
1-2 tsp. mirin, to taste
2 TBS. fresh parsley, minced
1/4 cup croutons, for topping, optional

directions

1. Heat the oil in a nonstick Dutch oven. Sauté the onions for
   20 - 30 minutes.

2. Add the kombu, sage, thyme and water. Simmer for 15 minutes.

3. Add the salt, shoyu, mirin and parsley. Simmer for 5 minutes.

4. Serve topped with croutons.

variation

- After step #3, pour the soup into oven-proof bowls. Top with mozzarella or Swiss-style tofu cheese. Bake or broil until melted.

baked croutons

ingredients

2 TBS. unrefined corn oil
1 pinch unrefined sea salt

1 pound sourdough bread, cut
   into 3/4-inch cubes

directions

1. Preheat the oven to 350°F.

2. Heat the oil in a nonstick skillet. Add the bread cubes and stir to coat with oil. Sprinkle with salt and place in a roasting pan. As an option, you can also add 1/8 teaspoon of ground oregano to the mix. Bake until slightly firm, 10 - 15 minutes. They will harden more as they cool, so don't overcook them.

3. Store in glass jars in the refrigerator or freezer.

fennel bisque

8 servings

Have you looked at fennel and wondered what to do with it? This soup is the answer. Fennel adds a hint of licorice flavor, which is complemented by garlic, basil and freshly grated nutmeg. Adapted from Lisa Turner's delightful cookbook, Mostly Macro.

ingredients

1 TBS. extra-virgin olive oil
1 medium onion, coarsely chopped
1/2 tsp. unrefined sea salt
2 garlic cloves
2 TBS. whole wheat pastry flour
4 cups water
1/2 tsp. Herbamere®
4 cups fennel bulb, coarsely chopped
1/4 tsp. white pepper
1 tsp. nutmeg, fresh, if possible
1/4 cup fresh basil leaves, thinly sliced

directions

1. Heat the oil in a nonstick skillet and add the onion and salt. Sauté until translucent, about 5 minutes. Add the garlic and sauté, stirring constantly for 1 minute.

2. Add the flour and sauté for 2 - 3 minutes, stirring constantly. Slowly add 4 cups of water and whisk until smooth.

3. Stir in the Herbamere® and fennel. Bring to a boil and cook over medium heat until the fennel is tender, about 15 minutes.

4. Add the white pepper and nutmeg. Transfer the soup to a blender and process until very smooth. Return the purée to the pot. Stir in the basil and simmer to marry the flavors, about 3 minutes.

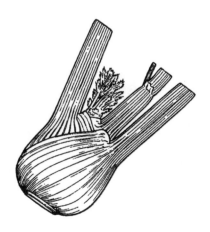

vegetable barley soup

10 servings

Many of the ingredients in this soup have soothing properties that calm the nervous system, making this soup a natural stress reliever.

ingredients

- 1 cup pearled barley
- 5 cups water
- 1 6-inch strip kombu
- 1/4 tsp. sesame oil
- 1 medium onion, diced
- 2 medium carrots, cut into 1/2 rounds
- 1/2 tsp. unrefined sea salt

- 3 cups buttercup or butternut squash, cut into 1/2-inch cubes
- 2 TBS. sweet, white miso
- 1 cup frozen peas, optional
- 1 TBS. scallions, thinly sliced, to garnish
- 1 sprinkle umeboshi vinegar per serving

directions

1. Add the barley and 5 cups of water to a stock pot. Soak for one to eight hours.

2. Bring the barley and water to a boil. Skim off foam from the surface until it subsides, about 15 minutes.

3. **Meanwhile,** cover the kombu with water and let soak for 5 minutes. Cut it into 1/2-inch squares and add it to the pot. Simmer for 1 hour with the lid ajar.

4. **Meanwhile,** heat the oil in a large, nonstick skillet. Sauté the onion until translucent, about 5 minutes. Move the onion to one side of the skillet and add a few more drops of oil to the cleared space. Add the carrots and the salt. Sauté for several minutes.

5. Add the squash and sautéed vegetables to the stock pot and cook until the vegetables are tender, about 15 minutes.

6. Place a small amount of the hot soup in a small bowl, add the miso, whisk until smooth and return it to the pot. Simmer for 2 minutes, then add the peas.

7. Serve garnished with scallions. Pass the umeboshi vinegar at the table.

variations
- Substitute parsnips for the carrots.
- For a creamy consistency, blend half the soup before adding the peas.

golden squash soup

10 servings

You can do a lot more with squash other than baking it with the usual butter and brown sugar. I love to add squash to soup. Buttercup is my favorite because it is so sweet! Its deep orange color is not only visually appealing, it's also high in beta carotene.

ingredients

7 cups boiling water
1 small buttercup squash
1 large onion, diced small
1 cup millet

3 TBS. sweet, white miso, or more to taste
2 TBS. fresh parsley, minced, to garnish, optional

directions

1. Bring 7 cups of water to a boil in a 4-quart pot.

2. **Meanwhile,** remove the blemished areas from the squash skin. Leave the remaining skin intact. Cut in half lengthwise, from top to bottom and scoop out the seeds. Trim away the stem and blossom ends and cut into 1/2-inch cubes. Set aside.

3. Add the squash and onion to the pot. Rinse the millet through a strainer and add it to the pot.

4. Place a flame tamer under the pot and reduce the heat to low. Cover and simmer until the soup becomes creamy, about 40 minutes. Stir occasionally.

5. Place a small amount of the hot soup in a small bowl, add the miso, whisk until smooth and return it to the pot. Stir and serve garnished with parsley.

variation
- Substitute butternut squash for buttercup.

cook's tip
- Leave the skin on vegetables to add fiber, texture and flavor to the soup. However, if you do not like squash skin, peel it off!

summer vegetable chowder

6 servings

This soup always gets rave reviews. The little-known fava bean is a gem floating in this perfect summer chowder.

ingredients

2 cups water
1/2 tsp. unrefined corn oil
1 medium onion, diced small
2 carrots, thin 1/2 rounds
2 celery stalks, diced small
1 garlic clove, minced
1 6-inch strip kombu
1 ear of corn, off the cob

1/2 tsp. dried basil
1 bay leaf
1/2 tsp. unrefined sea salt
1 pinch white pepper
8 pods fresh fava beans
2 TBS. sweet, white miso, or to taste

directions

1. Bring 2 cups of water to a boil in a 4-quart stock pot.

2. **Meanwhile,** heat the oil in a large, nonstick Dutch oven or skillet. Sauté the onion until translucent, about 5 minutes.

3. Move the onion to one side of the skillet and add a few more drops of oil to the cleared space. Add the carrots and sauté for about 3 minutes.

4. Repeat step #3 with the celery and garlic. Sauté them together for 1 minute, then add the contents of the skillet to the stock pot. Simmer, covered for 20 minutes.

5. **Meanwhile,** cover the kombu with water and let soak for 5 minutes. Cut it into 1-inch squares and add it to the stock pot. Add the corn, basil, bay leaf, salt and pepper.

6. **Meanwhile,** remove the fava beans from the pods and place in a bowl. Pour boiling water over them and let stand for 3 minutes to loosen the skin. Next, place the beans in a bowl of cold water. Use your thumb and first finger to rub off the bitter peel. Add the beans to the stock pot and simmer for 5 minutes.

7. Place a small amount of the hot soup in a small bowl, add the miso, whisk until smooth and return it to the pot.

variation

• Substitute 1 cup of canned fava beans or frozen peas for the fresh fava beans.

notes

creamy soups

To successfully create healthy, creamy soups, a blender is your best ally. Blending a portion of almost any soup creates a rich, velvety texture without added fat. To add extra creaminess, I like to include starchy vegetables and grains, such as yams, carrots, squash, parsnips, brown rice and rolled oats. Finally, I replace heavy, dairy products with a rich, smooth soy-rice beverage known as EdenBlend®.

A standard blender is the ideal appliance for creating an ultra-smooth consistency. Adding the soup in batches, one cup at a time prevents spillovers. Also, a damp dishcloth held over the top of a closed blender prevents the hot mixture from splashing out.

I often reach for my immersion blender, which goes right into the cooking pot to purée with little fuss. This tool shortens preparation and clean-up time and works best with vegetable soups. It does not, however, shred the outer skin of beans smoothly enough for bean soup.

A pressure cooker works especially well for creamy soups because it cooks the ingredients quickly and thoroughly. Thoroughly cooked ingredients can be easily blended to a smooth consistency. Creamy soups often thicken as they stand. You can add water to thin them and adjust the flavor before serving by adding shoyu to taste before serving. Don't worry if your soup comes out too thin, either. You can thicken it by whisking one teaspoon of kudzu or 2 teaspoons of cornstarch or arrowroot in 1/4 cup of cool water. Add it to the hot soup, return to a simmer and stir until it thickens, about 3 minutes.

Many of these soups can be used in combination with grain or noodles for a quick meal. Pour *Creamy Cauliflower and Chickpea Soup* over udon noodles, ladle *Double Chickpea Soup* over brown rice or millet, or serve *Indian Bliss Bisque* with white basmati rice.

See "All About Beans" for helpful information about their preparation, page 15.

the best broccoli soup

8 servings

This silky soup can be served as a quick, yet elegant lunch. Though it's missing the dairy, it's not missing the rich texture that you know and love. EdenBlend® beverage, a combination of brown rice and soy milk, lends non-dairy creaminess.

ingredients

1 tsp. unrefined corn oil
1 1/2 cups onions, cut into large pieces
3 stalks broccoli
1 bay leaf, in a tea ball
1 tsp. unrefined sea salt
2 tsp. shoyu

2 cups EdenBlend® beverage
1/4 tsp. dried thyme
1 pinch cayenne
1 small carrot, grated, to garnish, optional

directions

1. Heat the oil in a large, nonstick stock pot or skillet. Sauté the onions until translucent, about 5 minutes.

2. **Meanwhile,** cut off and discard the dried-out bottom of the broccoli stems. Peel the stems and coarsely chop. Separate the florets. Steam 1 cup of small florets for about 2 minutes and reserve them for the garnish.

3. Add the bay leaf, broccoli stems and remaining florets, salt and enough water to barely cover the vegetables. Cover and simmer for 10 minutes.

4. Discard the bay leaf and transfer the soup to a blender. Process until a creamy consistency is reached, adding more water if needed. Return the purée to the pot. Stir in the shoyu, EdenBlend® beverage, thyme and cayenne. Simmer for 5 minutes to marry the flavors. Adjust the seasoning by adding more shoyu to taste.

5. Serve garnished with grated carrot and the reserved broccoli florets.

variation
• Substitute another brand of soy or rice milk for the EdenBlend® beverage.

low-fat cream of broccoli soup

8 servings

Broccoli soup is traditionally made with loads of high-fat cream. I've created this low-fat version by substituting brown rice, which provides creamy body when blended.

ingredients

3 cups water
4 cups broccoli
1 small onion, cut into large pieces
2 1/2 cups cooked brown rice

2-4 garlic cloves
1/2 tsp. unrefined sea salt
3 TBS. sweet, white miso

directions

1. Bring 3 cups of water to a boil in a pressure cooker.

2. **Meanwhile,** peel the broccoli stems and coarsely chop them. Separate the florets. Steam 1 cup of small florets until tender, 2 - 3 minutes and set aside for the garnish.

3. Add the broccoli stems and remaining florets, onion, rice, garlic and salt to the pressure cooker. Lock the lid in place. Bring up to full pressure over high heat. Place a flame tamer under the pot and reduce the heat. Maintain high pressure for 10 minutes.

4. Quick-release the pressure.

5. Transfer the soup to a blender with the miso. Process until smooth, adding more water as needed. Serve each bowl garnished with 3 reserved florets.

variation

- Rather than pressure-cooking, simmer the soup in a stock pot for 20 minutes.

cook's tip

- I always make extra rice so I can make this soup with a minimum of fuss.

buttercup bisque

8 servings

A sweetness shines through this bisque that is subtle and nourishing. It's sinfully rich, yet low in fat. Be sure to top with toasted pumpkins seeds for the best effect.

ingredients

3 1/2 cups boiling water
1 medium buttercup squash, unpeeled, cut into large pieces
2 medium onions, cut into large pieces

2 TBS. sweet, white miso
1 TBS. toasted pumpkin seeds, to garnish

directions

1. Bring the water to a boil in a pressure cooker. Add the squash and onions. Lock the lid in place. Bring up to full pressure over high heat. Place a flame tamer under the pot and reduce the heat. Maintain high pressure for 15 minutes.

2. Quick-release the pressure.

3. Remove 2 cups of the cooking liquid and set aside. Add the miso to the soup. Using an immersion blender, blend the soup right in the pot, adding back liquid as needed to reach the desired consistency.

4. Simmer for 5 minutes to marry the flavors. Serve garnished with the toasted pumpkin seeds.

variation

- Instead of pressure-cooking, steam the squash for 20 minutes.

cook's tips

- See more about immersion blenders in "Essential Tools and Equipment."
- Use a standard blender in place of the immersion blender.

silken celery soup

4 servings

Rolled oats lend a creamy consistency to this easy-to-make soup. Serve with sourdough toast smothered in Almond Spread, *page 123.*

ingredients

1/2 tsp. unrefined corn oil
1 small onion, cut into large pieces
4 stalks celery, cut into large pieces
3 cups boiling water

1/4 tsp. unrefined sea salt
1/2 cup rolled oats
2-3 TBS. sweet, white miso
1 scallion, thinly sliced, to garnish

directions

1. Heat the oil in a nonstick Dutch oven. Sauté the onion until translucent, about 5 minutes. Add the celery and sauté for 2 minutes.

2. Add the 3 cups of boiling water, salt and oats to the pot. Simmer for 30 minutes, with the lid ajar, stirring occasionally.

3. Transfer the soup and the miso to a blender. Process until uniform in color. Return the purée to the pot and simmer for 5 minutes. Serve garnished with scallions.

variation

• Substitute 8 - 12 stalks of asparagus for the celery.

green split pea soup

8 servings

As a vegetarian, my mom left the ham out of this recipe. Job's tears, a wild barley seed, provides depth and richness instead. It is her favorite split pea soup and it may become yours as well!

ingredients

7 cups water	1 garlic clove, minced
12/3 cups green split peas	1 large carrot, cut into 1/2 rounds
3 TBS. Job's tears	1 celery stalk, diced small
1 6-inch strip kombu	1/4 tsp. dried basil
3 TBS. Job's tears	1/4 tsp. unrefined sea salt
1 large onion, diced small	3 TBS. shoyu, or to taste

directions

1. Bring 7 cups of water to a boil in a large stock pot.

2. **Meanwhile,** pick over the split peas to remove debris. Pick over the Job's tears for bits of black hulls. Add the rinsed peas and Job's tears to the pot and simmer uncovered for 15 minutes, skimming off foam from the surface until it subsides.

3. Cover the kombu with water and let soak for 5 minutes. Cut it into 1/2-inch squares and add it to the pot. Simmer 1 hour, with the lid ajar.

4. Add the remaining ingredients, except the salt and shoyu. Place a flame tamer under the pot. Simmer, with the lid ajar, until the split peas have completely dissolved, about 45 minutes. Stir from the bottom every 15 minutes to prevent the soup from scorching.

5. Add the salt and shoyu. Simmer for 5 minutes to cook the seasonings.

variation
- Substitute pearled barley for Job's tears.

cook's tips
- For more information about Job's tears, see the Glossary, page 151.
- When boiling bean soups, vent the pot by keeping the lid ajar. This prevents the soup from spilling over.
- Pea soup will thicken overnight. When reheating, add a little water.

purée of parsnip soup

8 servings

Have you ever cooked with parsnips? If not, you're in for a sweet surprise. Light miso rounds out the soup with its subtle, savory essence. Serve with crunchy, Homemade Sesame-Rice Crackers, *page 142.*

ingredients

- 1/2 tsp. unrefined corn oil
- 2 onions, cut into large pieces
- 1 pound parsnips, cut into large pieces
- 1 6-inch piece kombu
- 5 cups boiling water
- 1/2 cup rolled oats

- 1 bay leaf, in a tea ball
- 1 tsp. unrefined sea salt
- 3 TBS. chickpea miso
- 2 TBS. tahini
- 1 TBS. scallions, thinly sliced, to garnish

directions

1. Heat the oil in a large, nonstick Dutch oven. Sauté the onions until translucent about 5 minutes.

2. Add the parsnips and sauté for 5 minutes.

3. **Meanwhile,** cover the kombu with water and let soak for 5 minutes. Cut it into 1/2-inch squares and add it to the pot.

4. Add the 5 cups of boiling water, rolled oats and bay leaf to the pot. Place a flame tamer under the pot and simmer, covered, for 20 minutes. Stir occasionally.

5. Discard the bay leaf. Add the salt, miso and tahini. Transfer the soup to a blender in batches and process until smooth. Return the purée to the pot and simmer for 10 minutes. Serve garnished with scallion.

variation

- Substitute sweet, white miso for chickpea miso.

cream of shiitake soup

6 servings

This divine soup was inspired by a friend, Elaine King Gagné. Mirin, a natural rice wine, is used in place of sherry to balance the flavors. Although more involved than other recipes, it is worth the effort!

ingredients

10 dried shiitake mushrooms
4 cups water
1 6-inch strip kombu
2/3 cup rolled oats
3 TBS. shoyu, or more to taste

1/2 tsp. sesame oil
1 medium onion, diced small
1 TBS. mirin
1 TBS. fresh parsley, minced, to garnish

directions

1. Rinse the shiitake mushrooms and place them in a small bowl. Cover them with boiling water and steep to soften, about 20 minutes. Place a plate over the bowl to hold in the heat.

2. **Meanwhile,** add 4 cups of water and the kombu to a medium stock pot. Bring to a boil, then remove the kombu, reserving it for another dish.

3. Toast the rolled oats in a dry Dutch oven or skillet until golden brown, about 7 minutes. Add the oats to the stock pot and simmer covered for 30 minutes. Transfer the oat mixture to a blender and process until smooth and creamy. Return the purée to the stock pot.

4. **Meanwhile,** drain the mushrooms, straining the mushroom-soaking water into a measuring cup. Add enough water to total 1 cup and pour it into a small saucepan. Cut off the stems of the mushrooms and discard. Cut the caps into 1/4-inch slices and place in the saucepan. Add the shoyu. Simmer, covered, for 15 minutes, then add it to the stock pot.

5. **Meanwhile,** heat the oil in the nonstick Dutch oven or skillet. Add the onion and sauté for 5 minutes. Add the onion and mirin to the stock pot. Simmer, covered, until the onion and mushrooms are tender, about 20 minutes. Serve garnished with parsley.

variation

• Garnish the soup with thin strips of toasted nori in addition to the parsley.

cook's tip

• Refrigerate reserved kombu up to 4 days or freeze it for use in another dish.

creamy cauliflower and chickpea soup

8 servings

This mellow soup becomes spectacular when caramelized onions are sprinkled on top. For a quick lunch the next day, use leftovers as a sauce over rice or noodles. Serve with Homemade Sesame-Rice Crackers, page 142.

ingredients

1 cup dried chickpeas
2 1/2 cups water
1 6-inch strip kombu
1/4 tsp. sesame oil
1 small onion, diced small

1 large cauliflower, cut into large pieces
1/3 cup sweet, white miso
1 TBS. fresh parsley, minced, to garnish

directions

1. Pick over the chickpeas to remove debris and broken beans. Wash the beans and place them in a large bowl. Cover them with water, 2 inches above the level of the beans and soak for 24 hours.

2. Bring 2 1/2 cups of water to a boil in a pressure cooker. Add the rinsed chickpeas and return to a boil. Simmer uncovered for 10 minutes, skimming foam from the surface until it subsides.

3. **Meanwhile,** cover the kombu with water and let soak for 5 minutes. Cut it into 1/2-inch squares and add it to the pot.

4. Lock the lid in place. Bring up to full pressure over high heat. Place a flame tamer under the pot and reduce the heat. Maintain high pressure for 25 minutes.

5. **Meanwhile,** heat the oil in a nonstick skillet. Sauté the onions until caramelized, 15 - 25 minutes, the longer the better.

6. Steam the cauliflower in 2 cups of water until fork-tender, about 7 minutes. Set aside.

7. Quick-release the pressure. If the beans are tender, add the cauliflower and the miso. If not, simmer until the chickpeas are done.

8. Transfer the cauliflower, chickpeas and miso to a blender. Process until smooth, then return it to the pot. Heat through for several minutes to marry flavors. Serve garnished with caramelized onions and fresh parsley.

cook's tip

- The flavor of cauliflower is enhanced by steaming the entire head, whole, for 12 minutes before separating it into florets.

curried parsnip soup

8 servings

With a little imagination, plain parsnips are transformed into an Indian-style feast in this curried soup. Serve with Sesame Wheat Crackers, *page 141.*

ingredients

1/4 tsp. sesame oil
1 medium onion, into large pieces
1 1/2 tsp. mild curry powder
2 celery stalks, into large pieces
1 TBS. garlic, into large pieces
4 cups water
4 cups thin parsnips, into large pieces

3/4 cup rolled oats
3/4 tsp. unrefined sea salt
2 TBS. sweet, white miso
1 tsp. ginger juice
1 TBS. scallion, thinly sliced, to garnish

directions

1. Heat the oil in a pressure cooker over low heat. Add the onion and sauté until translucent, about 5 minutes.

2. Add the curry powder, celery and garlic. Sauté for 1 minute, stirring constantly.

3. Add the water, parsnips, oats and salt. Lock the lid in place. Bring up to full pressure over high heat. Place a flame tamer under the pot and reduce the heat. Maintain high pressure for 10 minutes.

4. Quick-release the pressure. Add the miso and ginger juice.

5. Transfer the soup to a blender and process until smooth. Return it to the pot and stir well. Serve garnished with scallions.

variation

• Serve garnished with carrot matchsticks.

cook's tip

• To juice fresh ginger, it must first be grated. A fine-tooth ginger grater works best. Place the shredded ginger in the palm of your hand. Squeeze the pulp over a strainer to prevent bits of pulp from falling into the soup. One tablespoon of grated ginger yields about 1 teaspoon of juice.

golden autumn soup

8 servings

The garnet yams and rolled oats create a lovely texture and visual appeal in this ambrosial soup. Be sure to add the parsley garnish for a bright splash of green.

ingredients

4 cups water

1 1/2 pounds carrots, cut into large pieces

1 1/2 pounds garnet yams, peeled and cut into large pieces

1 medium onion, cut into large pieces

1/3 cup rolled oats

1 tsp. curry powder, or more to taste

1 tsp. unrefined sea salt

1 TBS. shoyu, or more to taste

1 TBS. fresh parsley, minced, to garnish

directions

1. Bring 4 cups of water to a boil in a pressure cooker. Add the remaining ingredients, except the parsley.

2. Lock the lid in place. Bring up to full pressure over high heat. Place a flame tamer under the pressure cooker and reduce the heat. Maintain high pressure for 6 minutes.

3. Quick-release the pressure.

4. Transfer the soup to a blender and process until uniform in color. Serve garnished with parsley.

variations

- To minimize clean-up, purée the soup in the pressure cooker using an immersion blender in step #4.
- Add 2 large apples, peeled, cored and cut into large pieces, in step #1.

cream of mushroom soup

8 servings

Shiitake mushrooms add a wealth of healing properties to this soup, including reducing fat and cholesterol, enhancing the immunity and fighting carcinogens.

ingredients

18 dried shiitake mushrooms
7 cups boiling water
3/4 cup pearled barley
1/2 tsp. unrefined sea salt
1/2 tsp. unrefined corn oil
1 medium onion, diced small

2 medium garlic cloves, minced
3 TBS. shoyu
2 TBS. mirin
1 dash white pepper
1 TBS. scallions, thinly sliced, to garnish

directions

1. Rinse the shiitake mushrooms. Place them in a bowl and add boiling water to cover. Soak for 20 minutes, placing a plate over the bowl to hold in the heat.

2. Bring 7 cups of water to a boil in a 4-quart pot. Add the rinsed barley and the salt to the pot. Simmer, with the lid ajar, until the barley is tender, about 40 minutes.

3. Transfer 2 cups of the soup to a blender. Process until uniform in color and return it to the pot.

4. **Meanwhile,** heat the oil in a large, nonstick skillet. Sauté the onion until translucent, about 5 minutes.

5. Drain the mushrooms, reserving the soaking liquid. Cut off the mushroom stems and discard. Slice the caps into thin strips. Add the mushroom strips and garlic to the skillet. Sauté, stirring constantly for 1 minute.

6. Add the vegetables, strained mushroom soaking water, shoyu, mirin and white pepper to the soup.

7. Simmer until all the ingredients are tender, about 20 minutes.

8. Serve garnished with scallions.

indian bliss bisque

Mild sweet potatoes and cauliflower offer the perfect canvas for this melange of spices: ginger, curry, cumin, coriander and fenugreek. The mild sensation of jalapeño peppers adds the final touch in this delightful recipe adapted from Jay Solomon's Vegetarian Soup Cuisine.

ingredients

1 tsp. canola oil
1 medium onion, into large pieces
1 stalk celery, into large pieces
1 tsp. unrefined sea salt
2 garlic cloves, cut in half
1 small jalapeño, seeded and sliced in half
2 tsp. fresh, peeled ginger, into large pieces
2 tsp. curry powder

1 tsp. ground cumin
1 tsp. ground coriander
1/2 tsp. fenugreek
5 1/2 cups water
2 cups sweet potatoes, peeled, cut into large pieces
1 head cauliflower, cut into large pieces
2 TBS. scallions, thinly sliced, to garnish

directions

1. Heat the oil in a 5-quart, nonstick Dutch oven. Sauté the onion for 5 minutes. Add the celery, salt, garlic, jalapeño and ginger. Sauté stirring constantly for 1 minute.

2. Add the spices and sauté for 1 minute, stirring constantly. Add the water, sweet potatoes and cauliflower. Cover and simmer until the vegetables are tender, about 30 minutes. Stir occasionally.

3. Transfer the soup to a blender and process until a smooth consistency is reached. Serve garnished with scallions.

cook's tip

- I don't use garnet yams, as they are too sweet for this recipe.

cream of vegetable soup

6 servings

You can make this rich, yet dairy-free soup in about twenty minutes! The trick is cutting the vegetables into large pieces for fast preparation and compressing the cooking time to five minutes by using a pressure cooker. Eat as a soup or serve as a sauce over pasta or rice.

ingredients

- 2 cups water
- 1/2 rutabaga, peeled and cut into large pieces
- 1 small parsnip, into large pieces
- 1 onion, into large pieces
- 1 carrot, into large pieces
- 1/4 cup rolled oats
- 1 small turnip, into large pieces
- 3 leaves Chinese (Napa) cabbage, into large pieces
- 2 TBS. tahini
- 3 TBS. sweet, white miso
- 1 TBS. fresh parsley, minced, to garnish

directions

1. Bring 2 cups of water to a boil in a pressure cooker. Add all of the ingredients except the tahini, miso and parsley. Lock the lid in place and bring up to full pressure over high heat. Maintain high pressure for 5 minutes.

2. Quick-release the pressure.

3. Add the tahini and miso to the pressure cooker. Transfer the soup to a blender in batches. Process until a smooth consistency is reached. Serve garnished with parsley.

variation

- Simmer the soup in a stock pot for 20 minutes instead of pressure-cooking.

cook's tip

- For more information about rutabaga, see the Glossary, page 155.

double chickpea soup

6 servings

Leeks add a spring essence to this smooth chickpea soup. Note that leeks require special washing.

ingredients

1 1/2 cups dried chickpeas
4 cups water
1 6-inch strip kombu
1/4 tsp. sesame oil
1/2 cup minced leeks

1/2 cup carrots, matchsticks
1 1/2 TBS. tahini
1/4 cup chickpea miso
1 TBS. scallions, thinly sliced, to garnish

directions

1. Pick over the chickpeas to remove debris and broken beans. Wash the beans and place them in a large bowl. Cover them with water, 2 inches above the level of the beans and soak for 24 hours.

2. Add 4 cups of fresh water into a pressure cooker and bring to a boil. Add the rinsed chickpeas and return to a boil. Simmer uncovered for 15 minutes, skimming off foam that comes to the surface.

3. **Meanwhile,** cover the kombu with water and let soak for 5 minutes. Cut in into 1/2-inch squares and add it to the pressure cooker. Pressure-cook for 25 minutes.

4. **Meanwhile,** heat the oil in a large, nonstick skillet. Sauté the leeks and carrots for about 3 minutes. Set aside.

5. Quick-release the pressure. If the beans are not tender, replace the lid and simmer until the beans are done.

6. Transfer the soup to a blender. Add the miso. Process until a smooth consistency is reached, then return the purée to the pressure cooker. Add the sautéed vegetables and simmer until the vegetables are tender, about 10 minutes. Serve garnished with scallion.

variation

- Substitute sweet, white miso for the chickpea miso or a medium onion for the leeks.

cook's tip

- Leeks require special washing. Cut them in half, lengthwise, and wash layer-by-layer under running water to remove all the sand.

notes

international soups

Who doesn't love to experience other countries, even vicariously through their food? Recreating the soups of these cultures has a way of transporting you to another time and place. I never tire of expanding my horizons with new ethnic recipes. You'll find that I have a passion for lentil and split pea soups, partially because these beans do not require soaking and can be pressure-cooked in less than half an hour!

It is no wonder that most countries use nutritious and economical beans as a staple in their soups. Classic international favorites include black beans in Cuba, split peas in India, cannellini beans in Italy, adzuki beans in Japan and lentils in the Middle East. Regional recipes in the United States include red beans in New Orleans, navy beans in New England and black-eyed peas in the South. I hope you enjoy your culinary travels as much as I have!

See "All About Beans" for helpful information about their preparation, page 15.

cuban black bean

4-5 servings

Many of my students say that this is the best black bean soup they have ever tasted. This is undoubtedly because it evolved over many years of fine-tuning in my quest for perfection! I hope that you will enjoy it as much as we do. Be sure to place the bay leaf in a mesh tea ball so that you can easily remove it before blending.

ingredients

1 cup dried black beans
3 1/2 cups water
1 6-inch strip kombu, diced
1 bay leaf, in a tea ball
1 tsp. extra-virgin olive oil
1 large onion, diced small
3 garlic cloves, minced

3/4 tsp. ground cumin
1/2 tsp. ground oregano
1 tsp. mild chili powder
2 TBS. mirin
1 TBS. brown rice vinegar
2 tsp. unrefined sea salt
1 TBS. shoyu

directions

1. The day before, pick over the black beans to remove debris and broken beans. Rinse the beans and place them in a large bowl. Cover them with water, 2 inches above the level of the beans and soak overnight.

2. Bring 3 1/2 cups of water to a boil in a 6-quart pot. Add the rinsed beans and return to a boil. Simmer uncovered for 15 minutes, skimming off foam from the surface until it subsides.

3. **Meanwhile,** cover the kombu with water and let soak for 5 minutes. Cut it into 1/2-inch squares and add it to the pot. Add the bay leaf to the pot. Place a flame tamer under the pot. Simmer for 45 minutes, with the lid ajar.

4. **Meanwhile,** heat the oil in a large, nonstick skillet. Sauté the onion until translucent, about 5 minutes. Add the garlic, cumin, oregano and chili powder. Stir constantly for 1 minute. Scrape the contents of the skillet into the soup pot and simmer for 1 hour with the lid ajar.

5. Add the mirin, vinegar, salt and shoyu. Simmer for 15 minutes.

6. Remove and discard the bay leaf. Transfer 2 - 3 cups of the soup to a blender and process until uniform in color. Return the purée to the pot and stir. Serve garnished with scallions.

variation

- In step #2, pressure-cook the black beans for 10 minutes, then quick-release.

tuscan bean soup

8 servings

My students exclaimed, "Bravo," when they tasted this classic Italian soup, which is spiced to perfection. Serve with Italian bread and fresh salad.

ingredients

1 1/2 cups dried navy beans
   3 cups water
   1 6-inch strip kombu, diced
   1 tsp. extra-virgin olive oil
   2 carrots, 1/2 rounds
   2 celery stalks, diced
   2 garlic cloves, minced
   3 scallions, 1/4-inch slices

1 tsp. dried basil
1 tsp. unrefined sea salt
1 tsp. Herbamere®
1 dash white pepper
2 cups green beans into 1-inch pieces
1 TBS. fresh parsley, minced, to garnish, optional

directions

1. The day before, pick over the navy beans to remove debris and broken beans. Rinse the beans and place them in a large bowl. Cover with water, 2 inches above the level of the beans and soak overnight.

2. Add 3 cups of water to a 6-quart pot and bring to a boil. Add the rinsed beans and return to a boil. Simmer uncovered for 15 minutes, skimming off foam from the surface until it subsides.

3. **Meanwhile,** cover the kombu with water and let soak for 5 minutes. Cut it into 1/2-inch squares and add it to the pot. Place a flame tamer under the pot. Simmer until just tender, with the lid ajar, about 1 hour. Drain the beans, reserving the cooking water.

4. **Meanwhile,** heat the oil in a large, nonstick skillet. Sauté the carrots until tender, about 5 minutes. Add the celery, garlic, scallions and basil. Sauté, stirring constantly for 1 minute. Scrape the contents of the skillet into the soup pot.

5. Add the salt, Herbamere®, white pepper, green beans, drained beans and the reserved bean-cooking liquid to the pot. Cover and simmer until the vegetables are tender, about 10 minutes. Serve garnished with chopped parsley.

variation

- Substitute dried great northern beans or dried cannelini beans for the navy beans.

black bean soup with sun-dried tomatoes

8 servings

Italian and southwest flavors come together to form this amazing soup. Cumin, chipotle powder, cilantro and sun-dried tomatoes complement the earthy quality of black beans.

ingredients

2 cups dried black beans
5 cups water
1/3 cup sun-dried tomatoes, not packed in oil
1 cup water
1 6-inch strip kombu
1 tsp. extra-virgin olive oil
1 1/2 cups onion, diced small

3 garlic cloves, minced
1 tsp. ground cumin
1/2 tsp. chipotle powder
1 TBS. umeboshi paste
1 tsp. unrefined sea salt
1 TBS. barley miso
1/4 cup fresh cilantro, coarsely chopped

directions

1. The day before, pick over the black beans to remove debris and broken beans. Wash the beans and place in a large bowl. Cover them with water 2 inches above the level of the beans. Soak overnight.

2. Bring 5 cups of water to a boil in a pressure cooker. Add the rinsed beans and return to a boil. Simmer uncovered for 5 minutes, skimming off foam from the surface until it subsides.

3. **Meanwhile,** place the sun-dried tomatoes in a small bowl and cover with 1 cup of boiling water. In another bowl, cover the kombu with water. Let each soak for 5 minutes. Cut the kombu into 1/2-inch squares and add it to the pressure cooker.

4. Add the tomato-soaking liquid to the pressure cooker. Cut the tomatoes into thirds and add to the pressure cooker.

5. Lock the lid in place. Over high heat, bring up to full pressure. Place a flame tamer under the pressure cooker and reduce the heat. Maintain high pressure for 10 minutes.

6. **Meanwhile,** heat the oil in a large, nonstick Dutch oven. Sauté the onions until translucent, about 5 minutes. Add the garlic, cumin, chipotle powder and umeboshi paste. Stir constantly for 1 minute, then set aside.

7. Quick-release the pressure. If the beans are not tender, simmer until they are, then add the salt.

8. Add the beans and the bean-cooking liquid to the Dutch oven and gently stir. Place a flame tamer under the pot. Cover and simmer for 20 minutes. Stir occasionally to prevent sticking. Stir in the cilantro. Transfer 3 - 4 cups of the soup to a blender. Add the miso and process until smooth, adding water as needed. Return the purée to the pressure cooker and stir.

variations
* Substitute cayenne for the chipotle powder.
* In place of the dried black beans and 5 cups of water, substitute two 15-ounce cans of black beans, including the bean-canning liquid.

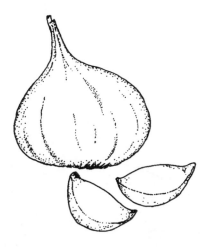

classic toscanini soup

4 servings

Legend has it that the famous conductor, Toscanini, ate this light soup before his concerts. If you would also like to have a light, but nourishing soup anytime, try this one! Sunflower Spread, *page 124, is a delicious accompaniment to naturally leavened bread.*

ingredients

1 tsp. unrefined corn oil
1/2 celery stalk, minced
4 cups boiling water
1/2 cup uncooked brown rice

1/2 tsp. Herbamare®
1 TBS. scallion, thinly sliced, to garnish

directions

1. Heat the oil in a nonstick Dutch oven. Sauté the celery for 1 minute.

2. Add the water, rice and Herbamare®. Cover and simmer until the rice is tender, 45 - 60 minutes. Serve garnished with scallions.

variation

- Substitute 1/4 teaspoon of unrefined sea salt for the Herbamere®.

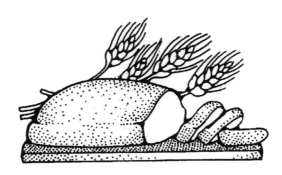

thai vegetable soup

8 servings

This vegetarian version of traditional Thai soup shines with jalapeño pepper and fresh ginger. It is sure to make it into your top ten favorite soups.

ingredients

- 6 cups water
- 1 TBS. grated fresh ginger
- 1 TBS. dried lemongrass, in a tea ball
- 1 jalapeño pepper, trimmed, seeded, cut into thin crosswise strips
- 2 small carrots, cut into 1/8-inch slices on the diagonal
- 2 stalks broccoli, cut into florets and the stalks into 1/4-inch slices
- 1/2 pound Napa (Chinese Cabbage), shredded
- 1/2 pound firm tofu, cut into 1/2-inch cubes, optional
- 1/4 cup tightly packed, fresh, minced cilantro
- 1/4 cup scallions, thinly sliced
- 2 TBS. shoyu, or to taste

directions

1. Bring 6 cups of water to a boil in a 4-quart pot. Add the ginger, lemongrass, jalapeño pepper, carrots and broccoli stalks. Return to a boil, then add the broccoli florets, cabbage and tofu. Cover and simmer until the broccoli is tender and crisp, about 3 minutes.

2. Remove the tea ball of lemongrass. Stir in the cilantro, scallions and shoyu. Simmer 1 minute before serving.

variation
- Substitute bok choy for the Napa cabbage.

cook's tip
- Wear rubber gloves when handling hot peppers.

hot and sour soup

4-6 servings

The enticing flavors in this soup are accentuated by adding a few drops of hot pepper sesame oil to each bowl.

ingredients

2 shiitake mushrooms
3 cups water
1 3-inch strip kombu
1/4 tsp. unrefined sea salt
1 1/2 cups Napa (Chinese) cabbage, shredded
1 5-ounce can sliced bamboo shoots, rinsed
1 tsp. brown rice vinegar

1 TBS. shoyu
2 TBS. arrowroot dissolved in 1/4 cup cool water
4 TBS. firm tofu, matchsticks, optional
2-3 drops hot chile sesame oil per cup
1 TBS. scallion, thinly sliced, to garnish

directions

1. Rinse the shiitake mushrooms. Place them in a bowl and add boiling water to cover. Soak for 20 - 30 minutes, covered with a plate. Cover the kombu with water and let soak for 5 minutes.

2. **Meanwhile**, bring the water to a boil in a 4-quart pot. Add the kombu and simmer for 2 minutes. Remove the kombu and reserve it for use in another dish.

3. Strain the mushroom-soaking water into the pot. Cut off the mushroom stems and discard. Cut the caps into thin strips and add them to the pot. Cover and simmer until tender, about 20 minutes.

4. Add the salt, cabbage, bamboo shoots, vinegar and shoyu. Simmer for 5 minutes.

5. Add the dissolved arrowroot and stir until thickened.

6. **Meanwhile**, place several pieces of tofu and a few drops of hot chile sesame oil in individual serving bowls. Pour the soup into the bowls and serve garnished with the scallions.

sizzling rice soup

4 servings

Sizzling Rice Soup *has been a staple in Chinese restaurants for years. Next time you plan to make your favorite stir-fry, start the meal with this healthy version of a classic soup. Your friends and family will be impressed with its authentic flavor.*

ingredients

2 dried shiitake mushrooms

1/4 tsp. sesame oil

1 1/2 cups cold, cooked brown rice

4 cups water

1 3-inch strip kombu

1 celery stalk, into large pieces

3 TBS. chickpea miso

1/8 tsp. unrefined corn oil

1 1/2 tsp. grated gingerroot, juiced

1 TBS. scallion, thinly sliced, to garnish

directions

1. Rinse the shiitake mushrooms. Place them in a bowl and add boiling water to cover. Soak for 20 - 30 minutes, covered with a plate.

2. **Meanwhile,** heat the sesame oil in a large, nonstick skillet. Crumble the rice into the skillet and sauté over medium-high heat, until golden and crunchy, about 30 minutes. Stir occasionally and set aside.

3. **Meanwhile,** bring the water to a boil in a 4-quart pot. Drain the shiitake and add it to the pot. Add the kombu and celery to the pot. Cover and simmer for 15 minutes.

4. Use a slotted spoon to remove and discard the kombu and all the vegetables, except for the shiitake. Remove the shiitake, cut off the stems and discard them. Slice the caps and reserve for use in another dish. Leave the stock in the pot.

5. Place a small amount of the hot soup in a small bowl, add the miso, whisk until smooth and return it to the pot. Add the corn oil and ginger juice to the pot and stir. Pour into individual soup bowls. Spoon the sizzling rice into each bowl and serve garnished with the scallions.

variations

- Add 2 - 3 drops of hot chile sesame oil to each bowl in step #5.
- Add a coarsely cut-up parsnip, carrot or onion in step #3.

moroccan vegetable soup

6 servings

Traditionally, Moroccan soup consists of zucchini, bell peppers, chickpeas, tomatoes and assertive spices. I have substituted canned chickpeas, which dramatically shortens the cooking time.

ingredients

1/2 tsp. extra-virgin olive oil
1 large onion, diced small
1 tsp. ground coriander
2 tsp. ground cumin
1 tsp. turmeric
5 cups boiling water
4 cups *Untomato Sauce*, page 147 or tomato sauce
1 15-ounce can organic chickpeas, drained

2 medium red bell peppers, diced small
1 1/4 tsp. unrefined sea salt
1/4 tsp. white pepper
2 small zucchini, cut into 1/4-inch 1/4 rounds
8 ounces orzo pasta

directions

1. Heat the oil in a nonstick Dutch oven. Sauté the onion, coriander, cumin and turmeric until the onion is translucent, about 5 minutes.

2. Add the boiling water, *Untomato Sauce*, chickpeas, red bell peppers, salt and white pepper. Simmer for 20 minutes, stirring several times, with the lid ajar.

3. Add the pasta, return to a boil, then simmer for 5 minutes. Add the zucchini and simmer until the pasta and zucchini are al dente, about 5 minutes. Serve hot.

variations

- Substitute 4 cups of chopped tomatoes for the *Untomato Sauce*.
- Substitute 2 cups of cooked chickpeas for the canned chickpeas.
- Substitute broken spaghetti for the orzo.

the ultimate lentil soup

16 servings

For many years I enjoyed this yummy soup at a Mediterranean restaurant in Arizona. I experimented and finally recreated it. I hope you enjoy it as much as I do. It freezes extremely well, so make the whole batch!

ingredients

4 cups green lentils
8 cups water
1 12-inch strip kombu
2 tsp. ground cumin
1 tsp. paprika
1/2 tsp. dried thyme
10 medium garlic cloves, minced
1/4 tsp. cayenne, optional

2 medium onions, diced small
2 bay leaves
3 celery stalks, diced small
3 carrots, cut into 1/2 moons
3 TBS. barley miso
1 TBS. unrefined sea salt
3 TBS. mirin
1 TBS. fresh parsley, minced, to garnish

directions

1. Pick over the lentils to remove debris.

2. Bring cups 8 of water to a boil in a large stock pot. Add the rinsed lentils and return to a boil. Simmer uncovered for 15 minutes, skimming off foam from the surface until it subsides.

3. **Meanwhile,** cover the kombu with water and let soak for 5 minutes. Cut it into 1/2-inch squares and add it to the pot. Simmer for 30 minutes with the lid ajar.

4. Add the remaining ingredients, except the miso, salt, mirin and parsley. Place a flame tamer under the pot. Simmer, with the lid ajar, until the lentils have completely dissolved, 3 - 4 hours. Stir from the bottom every 20 minutes to prevent the soup from scorching. Add water to thin the soup if it gets too thick.

5. Place a small amount of the hot soup in a small bowl, add the miso, whisk until smooth and return it to the pot. Add the mirin and salt and stir. Simmer for 20 minutes, then serve garnished with parsley.

variation

• Use red lentils to make this a crushed lentil soup.

festive tortilla soup

This rustic Mexican soup radiates the warmth of the sun. The preparation requires extra effort, but the results are well worth it. It is so hearty it can easily become a one-dish meal.

ingredients

5 cups water

1/2 tsp. unrefined corn oil

1 large onion, diced medium

1 cup cabbage, 3/4-inch pieces

1 cup carrots, 1/2-inch rounds

1 cup celery, 1/2-inch diagonals

1 TBS. mild chili powder

1 1/3 TBS. cumin powder

1 tsp. dried, ground oregano

1 TBS. unrefined sea salt

1 recipe *Peasant Beans*, page 65

1 quart *Untomato Sauce*, page 147 or tomato sauce

1-2 TBS. lemon juice, optional

1/2 recipe *Baked Corn Tortilla Chips*, page 140, cut into strips

1 scallion, thinly sliced, for garnish

1/4 cup cilantro, minced, for garnish, optional

directions

1. Bring 5 cups of water to a boil in a large stock pot.

2. **Meanwhile,** heat the oil in a large, nonstick skillet. Sauté the onion until translucent, about 5 minutes. Move the onions to one side of the skillet and add a few drops of oil to the cleared space. Add the cabbage and sauté for several minutes.

3. Repeat step #2 with the carrots. Repeat step #2 with the celery, spices and salt.

4. Add the vegetables to the boiling water and simmer for 30 minutes.

5. Add the cooked bean mixture, the bean-cooking liquid and the *Untomato Sauce*. Simmer for 15 minutes.

6. Just before serving, add the lemon juice and stir. Serve garnished with *Baked Corn Tortilla Chips*, scallion and fresh cilantro.

variations

• Top the soup with sliced, black olives.

• Serve additional *Baked Corn Tortilla Chips* on the side with your favorite salsa or guacamole dip.

peasant beans

8 servings

This simple, but tasty pot of beans is the foundation of many Mexican meals. Serve it as a soup, a side dish or use it as a filling in a burrito.

ingredients

2 cups dried pinto beans
4 cups water
1 6-inch strip kombu
1 onion, diced medium

2 garlic cloves, minced
1 tsp. unrefined sea salt
1 TBS. barley miso

directions

1. The day before, pick over the pinto beans to remove debris and broken beans. Rinse the beans and place them in a large bowl. Cover with water, 2 inches above the level of beans and soak overnight.

2. Bring 4 cups of water to a boil in a pressure cooker. Add the rinsed beans and return to a boil. Simmer uncovered for 5 minutes, skimming off foam from the surface until it subsides.

3. **Meanwhile,** cover the kombu with water and let soak for 5 minutes. Cut it into 1/2-inch squares and add it to the pressure cooker. Add the onion and garlic.

4. Lock the lid in place. Over high heat, bring up to full pressure. Place a flame tamer under the pressure cooker and reduce the heat. Maintain high pressure for 5 minutes.

5. Quick-release the pressure. If the beans are not tender, simmer until they are, then add the salt. Close the lid and let stand for 10 minutes, off the heat.

6. Place a small amount of the hot soup in a small bowl, add the miso, whisk until smooth and return it to the pot.

simple lentil soup

12 servings

This simplified version of the popular Mideastern soup is a great leftover for an impromptu lunch or dinner. Serve with wholesome bread and steamed vegetables.

ingredients

2 cups green lentils
8 cups water
1 6-inch strip kombu, diced
1 bay leaf
1/4 tsp. extra-virgin olive oil
1 onion, diced small
1 carrot, 1/2 rounds

1 celery stalk, diced
1 1/2 tsp. unrefined sea salt
1/2 tsp. ground oregano
2 TBS. barley miso
1 TBS. fresh parsley, minced, to garnish

directions

1. Bring 8 cups of water to a boil in a pressure cooker.

2. **Meanwhile,** pick over the lentils to remove debris. Cover the kombu with water and let soak for 5 minutes. Cut it into 1/2-inch squares and add it to the pot.

3. Add the rinsed lentils and return to a boil. Simmer uncovered for 15 minutes, skimming off foam from the surface until it subsides.

4. Place a flame tamer under the pot. Add the bay leaf. Simmer, with the lid ajar, for an hour.

5. **Meanwhile,** heat the oil in a large, nonstick skillet. Sauté the onion until translucent, about 5 minutes. Move the onion to one side of the pan. Add a few drops of oil in the cleared space and sauté the carrots and celery.

6. Scrape the vegetables into the soup pot. Add the salt and oregano. Simmer with the lid ajar, until the beans and vegetables are tender, 30 - 45 minutes.

7. Place a small amount of the hot soup in a small bowl, add the miso, whisk until smooth and return it to the pot. Serve garnished with parsley.

variation

• Add 1/4 teaspoon of cayenne in step #5.

classic mideastern soup

12 servings

I fell in love with this red lentil soup at a local, Mideastern restaurant. The pasta nests add a subtle, wholesome undertone that harmonizes with the curry. Serve with a big salad for a memorable, ethnic meal.

ingredients

2 quarts water
2 cups red lentils
1 6-inch piece kombu
1/4 tsp. extra-virgin olive oil
1 medium onion, diced small
5 medium garlic cloves, minced
1 tsp. mild curry powder
1 tsp. ground cumin
1 bay leaf

3/4 cup DeCecco® capelli d'angelo (pasta nests)
1 medium carrot, cut into thin 1/2 rounds
1 TBS. unrefined sea salt
2 TBS. sweet, white miso
2 TBS. scallions, thinly sliced, to garnish

directions

1. Bring 2 quarts of water to a boil in a large stock pot.

2. **Meanwhile,** pick over the lentils to remove debris. Place the lentils in a strainer and rinse thoroughly. Then, add them to the pot. Simmer uncovered for 15 minutes, skimming foam from the surface until it subsides.

3. Cover the kombu with water and let soak for 5 minutes. Cut it into 1/2-inch squares and set aside.

4. **Meanwhile,** heat the oil in a large, nonstick skillet. Sauté the onion until translucent, about 5 minutes. Add the garlic and spices. Sauté, stirring constantly for 1 minute. Scrape the contents of the skillet into the stock pot. Add the remaining ingredients, except the salt, miso and scallions to the stock pot.

5. Place a flame tamer under the pot. Simmer, with lid ajar, until the lentils are soft and creamy, about 1 1/2 hours. Stir from the bottom every 20 minutes to prevent the soup from scorching. Add more water if the soup becomes too thick.

6. Stir in the salt and cook for 10 minutes.

7. Place a small amount of the hot soup in a small bowl, add the miso, whisk until smooth and return it to the pot. Stir and serve garnished with scallions.

gingered lentil soup

12 servings

The inviting aroma of ginger makes this soup irresistible. Fingerhot chiles "kick it up a notch," as Emeril Lagasse says. Serve with whole wheat pita bread and a salad.

ingredients

2 cups brown lentils
7 cups water
2 6-inch strip kombu
1 tsp. canola oil
1 large onion, diced small
1 2-inch piece fresh ginger root, peeled and minced
1 tsp. ground coriander

2 green fingerhot chiles, diced small
2 tsp. curry powder
1/2 tsp. chili powder
2 tsp. unrefined sea salt
3 TBS. barley miso
2 TBS. fresh parsley, minced, to garnish

directions

1. Pick over the lentils to remove debris. Bring 7 cups of water to a boil in a pressure cooker. Add the rinsed lentils and return to a boil. Simmer uncovered for 5 minutes, skimming off foam from the surface until it subsides.

2. **Meanwhile,** cover the kombu with water and let soak for 5 minutes. Cut it into 1/2-inch squares and add it to the pressure cooker.

3. Heat the oil in a nonstick skillet and sauté the onion for 3 minutes. Move the onion to one side of the skillet and add a few drops of oil to the cleared space. Add the ginger, coriander, chiles, curry and chili powder. Sauté for 3 minutes. Add the contents of the skillet to the pressure cooker.

4. Close and lock the lid in place. Place a flame tamer under the pressure cooker. Over high heat, bring up to pressure. Then reduce the heat and maintain high pressure for 15 minutes.

5. Remove the pressure cooker from the heat and let stand for 15 minutes. Then, quick-release the pressure.

6. If the lentils are not soft, simmer until they are, then add the salt. Close the lid and let stand for 5 minutes, off the heat.

7. Place a small amount of the hot soup in a small bowl, add the miso, whisk until smooth and return it to the pot. Stir and garnish with parsley.

dashi with udon noodles

8 servings

You will probably make this soup for its time-honored flavor, but also appreciate shiitake's healing properties. According to traditional Asian medicine, it is anti-carcinogenic, helps reduce cholesterol and helps build the immune system.

ingredients

3 dried shiitake mushrooms
8 ounces udon noodles
6 cups water
1 3-inch strip kombu
3 TBS. shoyu

1/2 medium carrot, thinly sliced
1 1/2 tsp. grated ginger, juiced
2 snow peas, sliced into thirds on
the diagonal

directions

1. Rinse the shiitake mushrooms. Place them in a bowl and add boiling water to cover. Soak for 20 minutes, placing a plate over the bowl to hold in the heat.

2. Bring 5 quarts of water to a boil in a large stock pot. Cook the noodles until al dente, about 10 minutes.

3. Pour the noodles into a colander and rinse until cold. Leave them in the colander to drain.

4. **Meanwhile,** bring 6 cups of water to a boil in another stock pot. Add the kombu and simmer for 1 minute. Remove the kombu and reserve it for another recipe. Refrigerate it for up to four days or freeze it.

5. Remove the shiitakes, straining the shiitake-soaking water into the pot. Cut off the mushroom stems and discard. Cut the caps into thin strips and add them to the pot. Add the shoyu. Cover and simmer until tender, about 20 minutes.

6. **Meanwhile,** arrange the noodles in individual soup bowls. Blanch or steam the carrot slices until al dente, about 4 minutes. Place the carrots and snow peas on top of the noodles.

7. Remove the soup pot from the heat and add the ginger juice. Pour the broth and mushrooms into the bowls and serve hot.

variation

- Substitute scallions, sliced into 1-inch diagonals, for the snow peas.

yellow split pea dahl

10 servings

Dahl is an Indian term denoting a bean dish, usually prepared as a thick soup. Serve over basmati rice in the traditional style.

ingredients

2 cups yellow split peas	1 TBS. curry powder
6 cups water	3⁄4 tsp. fennel seeds
1 1/2 tsp. corn oil	1 /2 tsp. ground cinnamon
1 large onion, diced small	2 TBS. peeled, freshly grated ginger
1 6-inch strip kombu	1 bay leaf
2 celery stalks, thinly sliced	1 1/2 tsp. unrefined sea salt
1 1/2 pounds buttercup squash, diced small	3 TBS. sweet, white miso

directions

1. Pick over the split peas to remove debris and set aside.

2. Bring 6 cups of water to a boil in a large stock pot. Add the rinsed split peas to the pot. Simmer uncovered for 15 minutes, skimming off the foam from the surface until it subsides.

3. Heat the oil in a pressure cooker. Sauté the onion until translucent, about 5 minutes.

4. **Meanwhile,** cover the kombu with water and let soak for 5 minutes. Cut it into 1⁄2-inch squares and add it to the pressure cooker. Add the celery, squash, curry powder, fennel seeds, cinnamon, ginger and bay leaf to the pot.

5. Lock the lid in place. Bring up to full pressure over high heat. Place a flame tamer under the pressure cooker and reduce the heat. Maintain high pressure for 15 - 20 minutes.

6. Quick-release the pressure. If the peas are not soft, simmer until they are, then add the salt.

7. Close the lid and let stand for 10 minutes, off the heat.

8. Place a small amount of the hot soup in a small bowl, add the miso, whisk until smooth and return it to the pot.

variations
- To cook in a stock pot, simmer the split peas, with the lid ajar, for about an hour.
- Substitute green split peas or red lentils for the yellow split peas.

cook's tips
- For faster preparation, do not sauté the onion.
- A bay leaf flavors bean soups and helps reduce gas. A Boston tradition is to make a wish if you find the bay leaf in your soup bowl. It has a strong flavor, so do not eat it!

exotic red lentil dahl

12 servings

Wow your guests with this dahl. Sautéing the spices, also known as Indian magic, intensifies their exotic flavors. Adding squash lends a new twist to this classic.

ingredients

1 1/2 cup red lentils
1 tsp. unrefined corn oil
1 large onion, diced small
1 TBS. minced, peeled fresh ginger
1/2 tsp. ground cardamom
1/4 tsp. ground coriander
1 tsp. fennel seeds, crushed
1/8 tsp. ground cloves
9 cups boiling water

1 pinch asafoetida, optional
1/4 tsp. turmeric
1 3-inch stick cinnamon, in tea ball
1 6-inch strip kombu
1/2 small buttercup squash cut into
3/4-inch cubes
2 tsp. unrefined sea salt
1/4 tsp. white pepper

directions

1. Pick over the red lentils to remove debris and set aside.

2. Heat the oil in a large, nonstick Dutch oven or skillet. Sauté the onion until translucent, about 5 minutes. Stir in the ginger, cardamom, coriander, fennel seeds and cloves. Sauté for 1 minute, stirring constantly.

3. Bring 9 cups of water to a boil in a Dutch oven. Add the rinsed lentils and return to a boil. Simmer uncovered for 15 minutes, skimming off foam from the surface until it subsides. Then add the asafoetida, turmeric and cinnamon stick to the pot.

4. **Meanwhile,** cover the kombu with water in a small bowl and let soak for 5 minutes. Cut it into 1/2-inch squares and add it to the pot. Place a flame tamer under the pot. Simmer, with the lid ajar, until the lentils are tender and almost all dissolved, about 30 minutes.

5. Add the squash, salt and pepper. Simmer, until the squash is tender, about 10 minutes. Stir occasionally.

6. Remove the soup pot from the heat. Discard the cinnamon stick. Transfer 4 cups of soup to a blender and process until smooth. Return the purée to the pot and serve hot or cold.

variations
- Substitute butternut squash for the buttercup.
- Add 1 cup of chopped collards, kale or spinach to step #5.

cook's tip
- Asafoetida is available at most ethnic grocery stores.

mung bean dahl

This dahl is an easy way to include cauliflower in your cooking. The Indian spices wake up cauliflower's naturally mild flavor. Serve with Secret Sweet Potato Muffins, *page 136.*

ingredients

1 cup dried mung beans
5 cups water
1 3-inch strip kombu
4 garlic cloves, cut in half
1/2 tsp. ground cumin
1/4 tsp. cayenne

1 small cauliflower, cut into large
  pieces
1 1/2 tsp. unrefined sea salt
2 TBS. shoyu
1/2 carrot, matchsticks blanched, to
  garnish

directions

1. Pick over the mung beans to remove debris and set aside.

2. Bring 5 cups of water to a boil in a pressure cooker. Add the rinsed mung beans and return to a boil. Simmer uncovered for 5 minutes, skimming foam from the surface until it subsides.

3. **Meanwhile,** cover the kombu with water and let soak for 5 minutes. Cut it into 1/2-inch squares. Add it to the pressure cooker. Add the garlic, cumin, cayenne and cauliflower.

4. Lock the lid in place. Bring up to full pressure over high heat. Place a flame tamer under the pot and reduce the heat. Maintain high pressure for 15 minutes.

5. Quick-release the pressure. If the beans are not tender, simmer until they are. Then add the salt and the shoyu.

6. Close the lid and let stand for 5 minutes, off the heat. Serve garnished with carrot matchsticks.

cook's tip
- Pour this dahl over grain or vegetables as a hearty sauce.

split pea dahl

12 servings

Experience the fire of crushed red pepper flakes in this dish. Tear off pieces of warm, whole wheat chapati to scoop up this savory dahl.

ingredients

1 8-inch strip kombu	3/4 tsp. ground cinnamon
2 cups dried yellow split peas	6 large garlic cloves, minced
1 1/2 tsp. sesame oil	10 cups boiling water
1 1/2 tsp. cumin seeds	1/4 tsp. crushed red pepper flakes
1 1/2 tsp. mustard seeds	1 1/4 tsp. unrefined sea salt
1 tsp. turmeric	1/8 tsp. white pepper

directions

1. Cover the kombu with water and let soak for 5 minutes. Cut it into 1/2-inch squares and set aside.

2. **Meanwhile,** pick over the peas to remove debris and set aside.

3. Heat the sesame oil in a pressure cooker. Add the cumin seeds, mustard seeds, turmeric and cinnamon. Stir over low heat for 2 minutes. Add the garlic and stir constantly for 1 minute.

4. Slowly add 10 cups of boiling water, being careful not to get too close to the sputtering oil. Add the rinsed peas to the pot and return to a boil. Add the kombu and crushed red pepper flakes.

5. Lock the lid in place. Bring up to full pressure over high heat. Place a flame tamer under the pot and reduce the heat. Maintain high pressure for 20 minutes.

6. Quick-release the pressure. If the peas are not soft, simmer until they are, then add the salt and pepper.

7. Close the lid and let stand for 10 minutes, off the heat.

variation

• Rather than pressure-cooking, cook in a stock pot for about 2 hours.

creole pea soup

12 servings

Weak taste buds beware of this amazing pea soup! The Scotch bonnet pepper infuses the soup with a fruity and smoky flavor. It also adds anti-inflammatory and antioxident health benefits.

ingredients

3 cups yellow split peas
1 6-inch strip kombu
11 cups water
1 medium onion, diced small
2 TBS. chives, minced, optional
1 2-inch red chile or 1/2 Scotch bonnet, diced small
2 TBS. fresh parsley, minced

3/4 tsp. turmeric
1 1/2 tsp. dried thyme
1 TBS. unrefined sea salt
1/2 tsp. canola oil
1 tsp. whole cumin seeds
2 garlic cloves, minced
1 TBS. cilantro or scallion, minced, to garnish

directions

1. Pick over the split peas to remove debris.

2. Cover the kombu with water and let soak for 5 minutes. Cut it into 1/2-inch squares and set aside.

3. **Meanwhile,** bring 11 cups of water to a boil in a pressure cooker. Add the rinsed peas and return to a boil. Simmer uncovered for 5 minutes, skimming off foam from the surface until it subsides.

4. Add the kombu to the pressure cooker. Add the remaining ingredients to the pressure cooker except the salt, oil, cumin, garlic and garnish.

5. Lock the lid in place. Bring up to pressure over high heat. Place a flame tamer under the pressure cooker, then reduce the heat. Maintain high pressure for 15 minutes.

6. Quick-release the pressure. If the peas are not soft, simmer until they are, then add the salt. Let stand for 10 minutes, off the heat.

7. **Meanwhile,** heat the oil in a small, nonstick skillet. Add the cumin seeds. Let them sizzle for 10 seconds, then add the garlic. Sauté for 1 minute, stirring constantly. Add to the pressure cooker and stir. Serve garnished with cilantro or scallions.

curried red lentil soup

12 servings

Adapted from a recipe in World Vegetarian, *this soup stands apart from other lentil soups with the unusual addition of sweet potatoes. This makes it spicy and sweet at the same time.*

ingredients

- 2 quarts water
- 1 6-inch strip kombu
- 2 cups dried red lentils
- 1/2 tsp. extra-virgin olive oil
- 1 medium onion, diced small
- 2 garlic cloves, minced
- 2 tsp. fresh ginger root, peeled and coarsely diced
- 1 1/2 TBS. curry powder
- 1/4 tsp. ground cloves
- 1 large sweet potato, peeled and cut into 1-inch cubes
- 2 medium carrots, cut into 1/4-inch slices
- 2 tsp. unrefined sea salt
- 2 TBS. sweet, white miso

directions

1. Bring 2 quarts of water to a boil in a stock pot.

2. Pick over the lentils to remove debris. Place the lentils in a strainer and rinse thoroughly. Then, add them to the pot. Simmer uncovered for 15 minutes, skimming foam from the surface until it subsides.

3. **Meanwhile,** cover the kombu with water and let soak for 5 minutes. Cut it into 1/2-inch squares and add it to the pot. Add the rinsed lentils to the pot.

4. **Meanwhile,** heat the oil in a nonstick skillet. Sauté the onions until golden brown, about 10 minutes. Move the onions to one side of the skillet and add a few drops of oil to the cleared space. Sauté the ginger and garlic for 1 minute, stirring constantly. Add the curry powder and sauté for 10 seconds. Add the cloves, sweet potato and carrots. Sauté for several seconds.

5. Add the contents of the skillet to the pot. Place a flame tamer under the pot. Simmer with the lid ajar until the lentils are tender, about 45 minutes. Stir occasionally, adding water as needed.

6. When the lentils are tender, add the salt and miso. Simmer for 10 minutes.

7. Transfer the soup to a blender in batches and process briefly. The soup should not be completely smooth.

cook's tip

- Use a light-colored sweet potato. Garnet or jewel yams are too sweet for this recipe.

notes

hearty bean soups and stews

One question most vegetarians doubtlessly encounter is "How do you get enough protein?" The answer is simple – beans. And what better way to eat your beans than in soups and stews? You can make big pots of soup or stew over the weekend and add them to any meal throughout the week. This is an easy way to get that much-needed dose of amino acids.

What's more, bean soups and stews are a bountiful, economical source of protein, fiber, iron, calcium, B-1, zinc and niacin. They are also low in fat and have no cholesterol. Organic, dried beans are readily available in natural food stores and keep well.

See "All About Beans" for helpful information about their preparation, page 15.

creamy baked anasazi beans

6 servings

Nothing helps chase away the winter blahs better than a bowl of Creamy Baked
Anasazi Beans. *Fresh ginger root adds a lively contrast to the sweetness of anasazi
beans and barley malt syrup. Serve with* Herbal Corn Muffins, *page 133.*

ingredients

3 cups dried anasazi beans
5 cups water
1 6-inch strip of kombu
2 TBS. ginger juice

¼ cup barley malt
¼ cup brown rice syrup
3 TBS. barley miso
1 scallion, thinly sliced, to garnish

directions

1. The day before, pick over the anasazi beans to remove debris and
   broken beans. Wash the beans and place in a large bowl. Cover them
   with water, 2 inches above the level of the beans and soak overnight.

2. Bring 5 cups of water to a boil in a pressure cooker. Add the rinsed beans
   and return to a boil. Simmer uncovered for 5 minutes, skimming off
   foam from the surface until it subsides.

3. **Meanwhile,** cover the kombu with water and let soak for 5 minutes.
   Cut it into 1⁄2-inch squares and add it to the pressure cooker.

4. Lock the lid in place. Bring up to full pressure over high heat. Place a
   flame tamer under the pressure cooker and reduce the heat. Maintain
   high pressure for 8 minutes.

5. Preheat the oven to 325°F. Quick-release the pressure. If the beans are
   not tender, replace the lid and simmer until the beans are done.

6. Drain the bean-cooking liquid and set aside. Pour the beans into a
   3-quart baking dish.

7. **Meanwhile,** whisk together the ginger juice, barley malt, brown rice
   syrup and miso with 3 tablespoons of the bean-cooking liquid. Gently
   stir the sauce into the beans.

8. Bake uncovered for one hour. Add more bean-cooking liquid as needed.
   Served garnished with scallions.

spicy black bean chili

6-8 servings

On a chilly day, this chili will warm your soul. Chipotle peppers add their unique hot and smoky character. It becomes even more flavorful when refrigerated overnight. Complete the meal with a salad and Sweet Cornbread, page 129.

ingredients

2 cups dried black beans
1-2 dried chipotle peppers
1 6-inch kombu strip
2 tsp. extra-virgin olive oil
1 tsp. whole cumin seeds
1 large onion, diced medium
3-4 medium garlic cloves, minced
1 large red bell pepper, diced small
1 tsp. mild chili powder

1 tsp. ground oregano
1/2 tsp. whole fennel seeds
1/4 tsp. ground cinnamon
2 cups boiling water
1 tsp. unrefined sea salt
3 cups *Untomato Sauce*, page 147
  or tomato sauce
2 TBS. fresh cilantro, minced, to
  garnish

directions

1. Pick over the black beans to remove debris and broken beans. Cover the beans with water, 2 inches above the level of the beans and soak overnight.

2. Place the dried chipotle peppers in a bowl and cover with boiling water. Let stand for 60 minutes, covered with a plate. Wearing rubber gloves, drain off the water, remove the seeds and mince the peppers. Set aside.

3. **Meanwhile,** cover the kombu with water and let soak for 5 minutes. Cut it into 1/2-inch squares and set aside.

4. Heat the oil in a pressure cooker and sauté the cumin seeds over low heat until they begin to pop, 5 - 10 seconds. Add the onion and sauté until translucent, about 5 minutes. Add the garlic and red pepper. Sauté for 1 minute, stirring constantly.

5. Add the rinsed beans to the pressure cooker. Add the chili powder, oregano, fennel, cinnamon, chipotle peppers and the kombu. Immediately add about 2 cups boiling water to just cover the mixture. Stir well.

6. Lock the lid in place. Bring up to full pressure over high heat. Place a flame tamer under the pot. Maintain high pressure for 12 minutes.

7. Quick-release the pressure. If the beans are not tender, simmer until they are, then add the salt. Immediately, add the *Untomato Sauce*. Close the lid and let stand for 10 minutes.

8. Serve garnished with cilantro.

chili sans carne

8 servings

Who says chili without meat can't be fabulous? This dish will convince even skeptics that vegetarian chili measures up. Serve with Double Corn Muffins, *page 134, and a large salad to complete the meal.*

ingredients

1 cup dried kidney beans
2 cups water
1 6-inch strip kombu
1/2 tsp. canola oil
1 large onion, diced small
1 large celery stalk, diced small
6 garlic cloves, minced
1/2 tsp. ground cumin

1/2 tsp. mild chili powder
1 TBS. barley miso
1 1/2 TBS. barley malt syrup
3 cups *Untomato Sauce*, page 147
   or tomato sauce
2 TBS. scallions, thinly sliced, to
   garnish

directions

1. The day before, pick over the kidney beans to remove debris and broken beans. Wash the beans and place in a large bowl. Cover the beans with water, 2 inches above the level of beans and soak overnight.

2. Bring 2 cups of water to a boil in a pressure cooker. Add the rinsed beans and return to a boil. Simmer uncovered for 5 minutes, skimming off foam from the surface until it subsides.

3. **Meanwhile,** cover the kombu with water and let soak for 5 minutes. Cut it into 1/2-inch squares and add it to the pressure cooker.

4. Lock the lid in place. Bring up to full pressure over high heat. Place a flame tamer under the pressure cooker and reduce the heat. Maintain high pressure for 12 minutes.

5. Quick-release the pressure. If the beans are tender, set aside. If not, replace the lid and simmer until the beans are tender, then set aside.

6. **Meanwhile,** heat the oil in a large, nonstick skillet. Sauté the onion until translucent, about 5 minutes. Move the onion to one side of the skillet and add a few more drops of oil to the cleared space. Add the celery, garlic, cumin and chili powder. Sauté for 1 minute, stirring constantly. Transfer to the pressure cooker. Gently stir.

7. Place a small amount of the hot chili in a small bowl, add the miso and barley malt syrup. Whisk until smooth and return it to the pot. Add the *Untomato Sauce* to the pressure cooker and stir. Simmer, with lid ajar, to heat through and marry flavors, 20 - 30 minutes.

8. Serve garnished with scallion.

variations
- Substitute a different type of bean for kidney beans.
- Add 1 cup of seitan, cut into 1/2-inch cubes, to step #7.
- Add 1/2 pound sautéed, crumbled tempeh to step #7.

cook's tips
- This dish tastes even better the next day, after the flavors have further developed.
- Cook extra chili since it freezes so well. It makes a convenient meal when you are in a time crunch. Defrost in the refrigerator overnight.

double baked beans

12 servings

Bring these baked beans to your next picnic and watch them disappear. They're simple to make and resonate with a subtle, sweet flavor. Pair them with your favorite grilled veggie burgers and fresh corn on the cob.

ingredients

1 cup dried adzuki beans
2 cups dried black beans
8 cups water
1 12-inch strip kombu
2-3 TBS. fresh ginger juice, page 46

3-4 TBS. barley miso
2 tsp. unrefined sea salt
2 TBS. barley malt
1 TBS. scallions, thinly sliced, to
   garnish

directions

1. Pick over the adzuki and black beans to remove debris and broken beans. Wash the beans and place them in a large bowl. Cover them with water, 2 inches above the level of the beans and soak overnight.

2. Bring 8 cups of water to a boil in a pressure cooker. Add the rinsed beans to the pressure cooker and return to a boil. Simmer uncovered for 5 minutes, skimming off foam from the surface until it subsides.

3. **Meanwhile,** cover the kombu with water and let soak for 5 minutes. Cut it into 1/2-inch squares and add it to the pressure cooker.

4. Lock the lid in place. Bring up to full pressure over high heat. Place a flame tamer under the pressure cooker and reduce the heat. Maintain high pressure for 10 minutes.

5. Remove the pressure cooker from the heat. Let stand for 15 minutes, then quick-release the remaining pressure. This prevents the skins from coming off, while the beans continue to cook. Preheat the oven to 375°F.

6. Drain the beans, reserving 1 cup of the bean-cooking liquid in a 2-cup glass measure or bowl. Dissolve the ginger juice, miso, salt and barley malt in the hot bean-cooking liquid. Add the beans to a covered casserole dish. Pour the miso mixture over the beans.

7. Bake, covered, for 30 minutes. Remove the cover and bake for another 30 minutes. Serve garnished with scallions.

fabulous chipotle baked beans

8 servings

One of my absolutely favorite bean dishes, this smoky sensation will leave your guests asking for seconds. Add sautéed tempeh squares to step #9 for an even heartier dish. Then, top the meal off with fresh salad greens and Sweet Cornbread, page 129.

ingredients

2 cups dried navy beans
2 dried chipotle peppers
4 cups water
1 6-strip kombu, diced
1 tsp. canola oil
1 large onion, diced small

4 garlic cloves, minced
2/3 cups *Untomato Sauce*, page 147
   or tomato sauce
1/4 cups barley malt
1/4 cups brown rice syrup
1 TBS. barley miso

directions

1. Pick over the navy beans to remove debris and broken beans. Wash the beans and place them in a large bowl. Cover them with water, 2 inches above the level of the beans and soak overnight.

2. **Meanwhile,** place the chipotle peppers in a small bowl and cover with boiling water. Cover with a plate and soak for 1 hour. Discard the soaking water. Wearing rubber gloves, remove the seeds and mince the peppers with a knife or kitchen scissors. Set aside.

3. Bring 4 cups of water to a boil in a pressure cooker. Add the rinsed beans and return to a boil. Simmer uncovered for 5 minutes, skimming off foam from the surface until it subsides.

4. **Meanwhile,** cover the kombu with water and let soak for 5 minutes. Cut it into 1/2-inch squares and add the to the pressure cooker.

5. Bring up to full pressure over high heat. Place a flame tamer under the pot and reduce the heat. Maintain high pressure for 7 minutes.

6. Quick-release the pressure. Drain the beans, reserving the liquid.

7. Preheat the oven to 400°F.

8. Heat the oil in a Dutch oven. Sauté the onion and chipotle peppers for about 5 minutes. Add the garlic the last minute of cooking time.

9. Stir in the remaining ingredients, adding the beans last. If the beans look too dry, stir in some of the reserved cooking liquid. Bake, covered, for about 30 minutes, stirring occasionally.

macro baked beans

8 servings

This is a simple, classic baked bean recipe. Barley malt syrup is substituted for molasses, which is a sugar byproduct. Natural mustard adds a spicy touch. Serve with Macrobiotic Cornbread, page 130, and a leafy green vegetable.

ingredients

4 cups dried navy beans
8 cups water
1 12-inch strip kombu
1 tsp. unrefined sea salt
1/3 cup barley miso
1/4 tsp. canola oil
1 large onion, diced small

2 medium carrots, cut into 1/2 rounds
2 stalks celery, diced small, optional
4 garlic cloves, minced
3 TBS. prepared natural mustard
1/2 cup barley malt syrup

directions

1. The day before, pick over navy beans to remove debris and broken beans. Wash the beans and place them in a large bowl. Cover them with water, 2 inches above the level of beans and soak overnight.

2. Bring 8 cups of water to a boil in a pressure cooker. Rinse the beans through a colander. Add to the pressure cooker and return to a boil. Simmer uncovered for 5 minutes, skimming off foam from the surface until it subsides.

3. **Meanwhile**, cover the kombu with water and let soak for 5 minutes. Cut it into 1/2-inch squares and add it to the pressure cooker.

4. Lock the lid in place. Bring up to full pressure over high heat. Place a flame tamer under the pressure cooker and reduce the heat. Maintain high pressure for 6 minutes.

5. Quick-release the pressure. If the beans are not tender, simmer until they are, then add the salt. Drain the beans, reserving the cooking water. Pour the beans into a baking dish.

6. Pour a small amount of the bean-cooking water in a bowl and add the miso. Whisk until smooth, then pour it over the beans.

7. Preheat the oven to 350°F. Meanwhile, heat the oil in a nonstick skillet. Sauté the onion until translucent, about 5 minutes. Move the onion to one side of the skillet and add a few more drops of oil to the cleared space. Sauté the carrots and celery for 3 minutes. Add the garlic and sauté for 1 minute, stirring constantly.

8. Add 2 tablespoons of water to the skillet and cover. Steam until the vegetables are soft, about 3 minutes.

9. Add the vegetables, mustard and barley malt syrup to the beans and stir gently. Add the reserved bean-cooking liquid to barely cover the beans. Bake uncovered until golden around the edges, 1 1/2 - 2 hours.

cook's tip
• Rather then pressure cooking the beans, cook them in a large stock pot for about 1 1/2 hours.

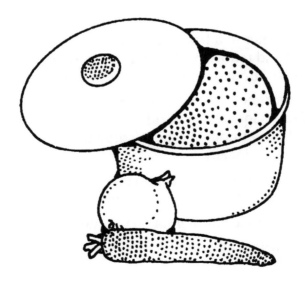

navajo bean stew

12-14 servings

In Navajo, anasazi means "ancient one." These maroon-and-white beans, indigenous to North America, have been used in cooking since 1100 A.D. Pinto beans, their close cousin, can be substituted, but note that the dish will not taste as sweet.

ingredients

1 1/2 cups dried anasazi beans	2 cups butternut or buttercup
6 cups water	squash, diced medium
1 6-inch strip kombu	1/2 tsp. dried rosemary
2 bay leaves	3 cups water
1 large onion, diced medium	1 tsp. unrefined sea salt
2 celery stalks, diced medium	1/4 cup shoyu
2 medium carrots, thick 1/2 rounds	2 TBS. scallion, thinly sliced, to
2 cups daikon, 1/4 rounds	garnish

directions

1. The day before, pick over the anasazi beans to remove debris and broken beans. Wash the beans and place them in a large bowl. Cover them with water, 2 inches above the level of the beans and soak overnight.

2. Bring 6 cups of water to a boil in an 8-quart stock pot. Add the rinsed beans to the pot and return to a boil. Simmer uncovered for 15 minutes, skimming off foam from the surface until it subsides.

3. **Meanwhile,** cover the kombu with water and let soak for 5 minutes. Cut it into 1/2-inch squares and add it to the pot with the bay leaves. Place a flame tamer under the pot. Simmer, with the lid ajar, about 15 minutes. Stir occasionally.

4. Add the vegetables, rosemary and remaining 3 cups of water to the pot. Cover and simmer until the beans are almost tender, about 15 minutes.

5. Add the salt and shoyu. Simmer for 10 minutes.

6. Serve garnished with scallion.

cook's tip
• Pass a bottle of balsamic vinegar or lemon wedges for added flavor.

native american casserole

8-12 servings

Squash, beans and corn were the traditional staples of Native American cooking. The combination of corn and beans is not only sumptuous, but it provides complete protein.

ingredients

1 cup dried kidney beans
3 cups water
1 6-inch strip kombu
1 medium onion, diced small
2 garlic cloves, minced
1 pound butternut squash, peeled and diced small

1/4 tsp. unrefined sea salt
1/4 tsp. mild chili powder or more to taste
2-3 ears of corn, off the cob
1 1/2 TBS. sweet, white miso
1 scallion, thinly sliced, to garnish

directions

1. The day before, pick over the kidney beans to remove debris and broken beans. Wash the beans and place them in a large bowl. Cover them with water, 2 inches above the level of the beans and soak overnight.

2. Bring 3 cups of water to a boil in a pressure cooker. Add the rinsed beans and return to a boil. Simmer uncovered for 5 minutes, skimming off foam from the surface until it subsides.

3. **Meanwhile,** cover the kombu with water and soak for 5 minutes. Cut it into 1/2-inch squares and add it to the pressure cooker.

4. Lock the lid in place. Bring up to full pressure over high heat. Place a flame tamer under the pressure cooker and reduce the heat. Maintain high pressure for 10 minutes.

5. Quick-release the pressure. Drain the beans, reserving the cooking liquid.

6. Place the onion, garlic and squash in a Dutch oven. Add the beans, salt, chili powder and 1 inch of bean-cooking liquid to the pot. Cover and simmer until the vegetables are tender, about 20 minutes.

7. Add the corn and simmer 10 minutes.

8. With the lid ajar, cook off excess liquid until a thick, stew-like consistency is reached.

9. Pour a small amount of the hot cooking liquid in a bowl and add the miso. Whisk until smooth, then return to the pot. Serve garnished with scallions.

spicy black-eyed pea stew

8 servings

This Greek-style stew will tease your palate. Its lemon-infused flavor is accented by occasional flashes of heat from the jalapeño peppers. Humble black-eyed peas cook quickly and require no soaking.

ingredients

2 1/2 cups dried black-eyed peas
5 cups water
1 6-inch strip kombu
2 tsp. extra-virgin olive oil
1 large onion, diced small
3 fresh jalapeño peppers, seeded and minced
2 garlic cloves, minced
1 tsp. lemon rind
1/2 tsp. white pepper

1/2 tsp. dried oregano
1 1/2 tsp. garlic powder
1/4 tsp. ground fennel
1/2 tsp. cinnamon
1/2 tsp. nutmeg
2 bay leaves, in a tea ball
1 TBS. unrefined sea salt
1 red bell pepper, diced small
1 TBS. fresh parsley, minced

directions

1. Pick over the black-eyed peas to remove debris and broken peas. Wash the peas and place them in a large bowl. Cover them with water, 2 inches above the level of the peas and soak for 1 hour.

2. Bring 5 cups of water to a boil in a 6-quart stockpot. Add the rinsed peas and return to a boil. Simmer uncovered for 15 minutes, skimming off foam from the surface until it subsides.

3. **Meanwhile,** cover the kombu with water and let soak for 5 minutes. Cut it into 1/2-inch squares and add it to the pot.

4. **Meanwhile,** heat the oil in a large, nonstick skillet. Sauté the onions for about 3 minutes. Add the jalapeños and sauté for 3 minutes. Move the vegetables to one side of the skillet and add a few more drops of oil to the cleared space. Sauté the garlic for 1 minute and add all to the pot.

5. Add the remaining ingredients except the salt, red bell pepper and parsley. Place a flame tamer under the pot and reduce the heat. Simmer, with the lid ajar, until the peas are just tender, about 45 minutes. Add water, as needed, to cover the peas. Stir occasionally.

6. Add the salt, red bell pepper and parsley. Simmer for 15 minutes, stirring several times.

sweet adzuki bean stew

6 servings

This stew is a traditional Japanese remedy for hypoglycemia. The squash nourishes the pancreas, stabilizing the blood sugar. If you are desperately seeking crunch in your meals, pile on some homemade Sesame Wheat Crackers, *page 141.*

ingredients

1 cup dried adzuki beans
1 6-inch strip kombu
1 tsp. unrefined sea salt

1 cup butternut squash, diced small
1 TBS. scallion, thinly sliced, to garnish

directions

1. Pick over the adzuki beans to remove debris and broken beans. Wash the beans and place them in a large bowl. Cover them with water, 2 inches above the level of beans and soak overnight.

2. Cover the kombu with water and let soak for 5 minutes. Cut it into 1/2-inch squares and add to a small Dutch oven.

3. Add the rinsed beans to the pot with enough water to just cover them. Bring to a boil and place a flame tamer under the pot. Cover and simmer for about 45 minutes, adding more water as needed to barely cover the beans.

4. When the beans are almost tender, add the salt and stir gently. Add 2 inches of water to the bottom of the pot. Place the squash on top of the beans, but do not stir. Simmer until the squash is fork-tender, 20 - 30 minutes.

5. Mix gently and serve garnished with scallions.

savory adzuki casserole

8-10 servings

This casserole is reminiscent of a corned beef sandwich with mustard. It makes a hearty centerpiece for a cold winter's meal.

ingredients

2 cups dried adzuki beans	1 tsp. caraway seeds
3 3/4 cups water	2 TBS. prepared natural mustard
1 6-inch strip kombu	2 garlic cloves, minced
1 tsp. barley miso	1/4 tsp. black pepper
2 cups sauerkraut, drained	

directions

1. The day before, pick over the adzuki beans to remove debris and broken beans. Wash the beans and place in a large bowl. Cover them with water, 2 inches above the level of the beans and soak overnight.

2. Bring 3 3/4 cups of water to a boil in a pressure cooker. Add the rinsed beans and return to a boil. Simmer uncovered for about 5 minutes, skimming off the foam that comes to the surface.

3. **Meanwhile,** cover the kombu with water and let soak for 5 minutes. Cut it into 1/2-inch squares and add it to the pressure cooker.

4. Lock the lid in place. Bring up to full pressure over high heat. Place a flame tamer under the pressure cooker and reduce the heat. Maintain high pressure for 15 minutes.

5. Quick-release the pressure. If the beans are not tender, simmer until they are, then add the miso.

6. Preheat the oven to 350°F.

7. Mash half the beans with a potato masher. Add the remaining ingredients to the pressure cooker and stir to combine. Spoon the mixture into a baking dish and bake, uncovered, until the flavors marry, 20 - 30 minutes.

pinto barley stew

10 servings

This stew is gratifying any time of day. It even makes a wholesome breakfast that will hold you comfortably until lunch.

ingredients

1 cup dried pinto beans
1/2 cups pearled barley
1 tsp. dark sesame oil
1 large onion, diced small
2 carrots, 1/2 rounds
1 celery stalk, diced small

3 cups boiling water
1 6-inch strip kombu
1 tsp. unrefined sea salt
2 TBS. shoyu
2 TBS. scallions, thinly sliced, to garnish

directions

1. The day before, pick over the pinto beans to remove debris and broken beans. Wash the beans and place them in a large bowl. Cover them with water, 2 inches above the level of the beans and soak overnight. Soak the barley in 3 cups of water in another bowl.

2. Heat the oil in a pressure cooker over low heat. Add the onion and sauté until translucent, about 5 minutes.

3. Add the rinsed beans, carrots, celery and boiling water to the pressure cooker. Return to a boil.

4. **Meanwhile,** cover the kombu with water and let soak for 5 minutes. Cut it into 1/2-inch squares and add it to the pressure cooker. Add the barley and the barley-soaking water to the pressure cooker.

5. Lock the lid in place. Bring up to full pressure over high heat. Place a flame tamer under the pressure cooker and reduce the heat. Maintain high pressure for 5 minutes.

6. Quick-release the pressure. If the beans are not tender, simmer until they are, then add the salt and shoyu.

7. Close the lid and let stand for 10 minutes, off the heat. Serve garnished with scallions.

variation

• Substitute kidney beans for pinto beans.

black soybean stew

4 servings

Black soybeans are surprisingly sweet and delicious. They are also reputed to nourish the female reproductive organs. Serve with Wheat-Free Muffins, *page 139, for a completely guilt-free meal.*

ingredients

1 cup dried black soybeans
1⁄4 tsp. unrefined sea salt
1 6-inch strip kombu
1 tsp. sesame oil
1 medium onion, diced small
1 carrot, 1⁄4-inch rounds

1 stalk burdock, thin rounds
1 1⁄2-inch piece fresh ginger, grated and juiced, page 46
2 TBS. brown rice miso
1 TBS. scallion, thinly sliced, to garnish

directions

1. Pick over the soybeans to remove debris and broken beans. Wash the beans and place them in a large bowl. Cover them with water, 2 inches above the level of the beans. Add salt to keep the skins from coming off during cooking. Soak overnight.

2. Blot the beans in the morning with paper towels to remove excess salty water. Add the beans to a medium Dutch oven and add enough boiling water to just cover them. Simmer uncovered for 15 minutes, skimming off foam from the surface until it subsides.

3. **Meanwhile,** cover the kombu with water and let soak for 5 minutes. Cut it into 1⁄2-inch squares and add to the pot. Simmer with the lid ajar, for about 2 hours. Stir occasionally, adding water as needed to cover the beans.

4. **Meanwhile,** heat the oil in a large, nonstick skillet. Sauté the onion until translucent, about 5 minutes. Move the onion to one side of the skillet and add a few drops of oil to the cleared space. Sauté the carrot and burdock for 4 minutes. Add the vegetables to the beans after the beans have cooked for 2 hours.

5. Continue to simmer the stew, with the lid ajar, until the beans are tender, an additional 3 - 4 hours, adding water as needed.

6. Place a small amount of the hot stew in a small bowl, add the miso, whisk until smooth and return it to the pot. Add the ginger juice serve garnished with scallions.

variation
- Add one 15-ounce can of Eden® Black Soy Beans to step #4 to substitute for the dried soy beans. Cook the stew for a total of 1 hour.

cook's tips
- Dried, organic black soybeans are available at Gold Mine Natural Foods. See Mail Order Sources, page 166.
- To juice fresh ginger, it must first be grated. A fine-toothed ginger grater works best. Place the shredded pulp in the palm of your hand and squeeze the juice through a strainer. One tablespoon of grated ginger yields about 1 teaspoon of juice.

chickpea stew

8 servings

This soup quickly became a student favorite at my cooking school. It is so substantial that you can use it as a sauce over rice or noodles. Serve with steamed green vegetables to complete the meal. Pressure-cooking chickpeas saves a lot of time.

ingredients

3⁄4 cup dried chickpeas
2 cups water
1 6-inch strip kombu
1⁄4 tsp. unrefined corn oil
2 medium onions, diced
4 celery stalks, diced

2 TBS. shoyu
2 TBS. tahini
1 cup butternut squash, diced
1 tsp. unrefined sea salt
1 TBS. fresh parsley, minced, to garnish

directions

1. The day before, pick over the chickpeas to remove debris and broken beans. Wash the beans and place them in a large bowl. Cover them with water, 2 inches above the level of beans and soak overnight.

2. Bring 2 cups of water to a boil in a pressure cooker. Add the rinsed chickpeas and return to a boil. Simmer uncovered for 5 minutes, skimming off foam that comes to the surface.

3. **Meanwhile,** cover the kombu with water and let soak for 5 minutes. Cut it into 1⁄2-inch squares and add it to the pressure cooker.

4. Lock the lid in place. Bring up to full pressure over high heat. Place a flame tamer under the pressure cooker and reduce the heat. Maintain high pressure for 25 minutes.

5. **Meanwhile,** heat the oil in a nonstick skillet. Sauté the onions until slightly brown, about 15 minutes. Move the onions to one side of the pan and add a few more drops of oil to the cleared space. Sauté the celery for 1 minute.

6. Whisk together the shoyu and tahini in a small bowl and set aside.

7. Quick-release the pressure. Add the onions, celery and squash.

8. If the beans are not tender, simmer until they are. Then add the salt and the tahini-shoyu mixture. Close the lid and let stand for 5 minutes, off the heat. Serve garnished with parsley.

navy bean chowder

10 servings

If you do not have a navy bean soup in your repertoire, this is the one for you. Don't be daunted by the number of steps. The results are well worth it.

ingredients

1 cup dried navy beans
6 cups water
4 ears of corn, off the cob
1 6-inch strip wakame
1 tsp. unrefined sea salt
1/2 tsp. unrefined corn oil

1 large onion, diced small
1 carrot, 1/2 rounds
1 celery stalk, diced small
3-4 TBS. sweet, white miso
1 scallion, thinly sliced, to garnish

directions

1. The day before, pick over the navy beans to remove debris and broken beans. Wash the beans and place them in a large bowl. Cover them with water, 2 inches above the level of the beans and soak overnight.

2. Bring 6 cups of water to a boil in a pressure cooker. **Meanwhile,** cut the corn off the cob and set the kernels aside. Add the corn cobs to the boiling water and simmer covered, for 10 minutes, then discard the cobs.

3. **Meanwhile,** cover the wakame with water and soak for 5 minutes. Cut it into 1/2-inch squares and add it to the pressure cooker with the rinsed beans.

4. Lock the lid in place. Bring up to full pressure over high heat. Place a flame tamer under the pressure cooker and reduce the heat. Maintain full pressure for 10 minutes.

5. Quick-release the pressure. If the beans are not tender, simmer until they are, then add the salt.

6. **Meanwhile,** heat the oil in a large, nonstick skillet. Sauté the onion until translucent. Move the onion to one side of the skillet and add a few more drops of oil to the cleared space. Sauté the carrot for 3 minutes and add them to the pressure cooker. Simmer 15 minutes.

7. Add the corn and celery. Simmer for 5 minutes.

8. Place a small amount of the hot chowder in a small bowl, add the miso, whisk until smooth and return it to the pressure cooker. Stir and serve garnished with scallions.

red lentil corn chowder

10 servings

For years, this has been the favorite soup of my beginning students. Most tell me that even their meat-and-potato eaters love it!

ingredients

6 cups water
1 cup red lentils
2 ears of corn, husked
1 6-inch strip kombu
1/2 tsp. unrefined corn oil
1 medium onion, diced small

2 carrots, cut into rounds,
   1/4-inch thick
3 celery stalks, diced small
3 TBS. sweet, white miso
1 TBS. fresh parsley, minced, to
   garnish, optional

directions

1. Bring 6 cups of water to a boil in a large stock pot.
2. **Meanwhile,** pick over the lentils to remove debris and set aside.
3. Add the corn to the stock pot and boil for 10 minutes. This makes a simple, sweet soup stock. Remove the cobs and allow to cool. Cut the kernels off the cobs and set aside. Discard the cobs.
4. Add the rinsed lentils to the pot. Simmer uncovered for 15 minutes, skimming off foam from the surface until it subsides.
5. **Meanwhile,** cover the kombu with water and let soak for 5 minutes. Cut it into 1/2-inch squares and add it to the pot.
6. Heat the oil in a large, nonstick skillet. Sauté the onion until translucent, about 5 minutes. Move the onion to one side of the skillet and add a few more drops of oil to the cleared space. Add the carrots and sauté for several minutes. Repeat with the celery. Add all the vegetables to the stock pot.
7. Place a flame tamer under the pot. Simmer, with the lid ajar, until the lentils are soft and creamy, about 45 minutes. Stir occasionally.
8. Place a small amount of the hot chowder in a small bowl, add the miso, whisk until smooth and return it to the pot. Stir and serve garnished with parsley.

variation

- Substitute sweet, white miso for the chickpea miso.

cook's tips

- Lay the corn cob horizontally on the board to slice off kernels to minimize clean-up.
- Use a Bash 'N Chop® to efficiently scoop up corn kernels and other vegetables.

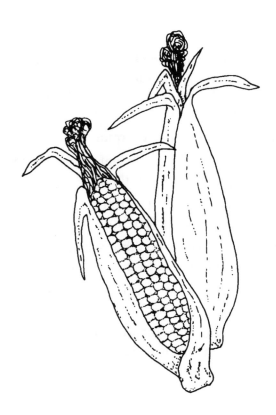

chickpea chowder

16 servings

The combination of chickpeas and tahini creates a creamy, hearty soup. An added bonus is the high amount of calcium from the tahini. Serve with Macrobiotic Cornbread, *page 130, for a meal that is sure to please your whole family.*

ingredients

2 cups dried chickpeas
1/2 cup pearled barley
5 cups water
1 6-inch strip kombu, squares
2 medium onions, diced medium
1 large butternut squash, peeled
and diced into 1/2-inch squares

1/4 cup tahini
4 carrots, sliced
1/2 small cabbage, diced
1 tsp. unrefined sea salt
1/4 cup chickpea miso
2 TBS. fresh parsley, minced, to
garnish

directions

1. The day before, pick over the chickpeas to remove debris and broken beans. Wash the beans and place them in a large bowl. Cover them with water, 2 inches above the level of the beans and soak overnight. Place the barley in another bowl and cover with 2 cups of water.

2. Bring 5 cups of water to a boil in a 4-quart pot.

3. **Meanwhile,** cover the kombu with water and let soak for 5 minutes. Cut it into 1/2-inch squares add it to the pot.

4. Add the rinsed beans to the pot. Simmer uncovered for 15 minutes, skimming off foam from the surface until it subsides.

5. Add the barley and the barley-soaking water to the pot. Place a flame tamer under the pot. Simmer, with the lid ajar, for about 1 1/2 hours.

6. Add the onions, squash, tahini, carrots, cabbage and salt. Simmer for another 1 1/2 hours.

7. Transfer 4 cups of the soup to a blender and add the miso. Process until uniform in color, then return it to the pot. Add more salt or miso, to taste. Serve garnished with parsley.

variation

*   Instead of stovetop cooking the chickpeas and vegetables in steps #3 and #4, pressure-cook them for 25 minutes, then quick-release.

classic northern bean soup

12 servings

Pressure-cooking this recipe takes considerably less time than boiling. Serve with Sesame Wheat Crackers, page 141.

ingredients

2 cups dried great northern beans
6 cups water
1 6-inch strip kombu
1 bay leaf
1 large onion, diced small
2 carrots, diced small

2 celery stalks, thinly sliced
1/4 tsp. dried thyme
2 tsp. unrefined sea salt
2 TBS. fresh parsley, minced, to garnish

directions

1. The day before, pick over the northern beans to remove debris and broken beans. Wash the beans and place them in a large bowl. Cover them with water, 2 inches above the level of the beans and soak overnight.

2. Bring 6 cups of water to a boil in a pressure cooker. Add the rinsed beans to the pressure cooker and return to a boil. Simmer uncovered for 5 minutes, skimming off foam from the surface until it subsides.

3. **Meanwhile,** cover the kombu with water and let soak for 5 minutes. Cut it into 1/2-inch squares and add it to the pressure cooker. Add the bay leaf, onion, carrots, celery and thyme.

4. Lock it in place. Bring up to high pressure over high heat. Place a flame tamer under the pressure cooker and reduce the heat. Maintain high pressure for 5 minutes.

5. Quick-release the pressure. If the beans are not tender, simmer until they are, then add the salt.

6. Close the lid and let stand for 5 minutes, off the heat. Serve garnished with parsley.

variations

- To cook in a stock pot, simmer, covered, about an hour.
- For a rich flavor, sauté the onions, carrots and celery in 1/2 teaspoon of canola oil in step #3, before adding to the beans.
- For a creamy consistency, blend 3 cups of the soup before serving.

traditional navy bean soup

14 servings

This is a great, basic spring soup. It is terrific served with Southern-Style Biscuits, *page 128.*

ingredients

2 cups dried navy beans
7 cups water
2 6-inch strips wakame
3 bay leaves
1 tsp. extra-virgin olive oil
1 large onion, diced

2 large leeks, diced
2 tsp. unrefined sea salt
1/3 cup sweet, white miso
1 small carrot, grated and steamed
for garnish

directions

1. The day before pick over the navy beans to remove debris, and broken beans. Wash the beans and place them in a large bowl. Cover them with water 2 inches above the level of the beans and soak overnight.

2. Bring 7 cups of water to a boil in a pressure cooker. Add the rinsed beans to the pressure cooker and return to a boil. Simmer uncovered for 5 minutes, skimming the foam from the surface until it subsides.

3. **Meanwhile,** cover the wakame with water and soak for 5 minutes. Cut it into 1/2-inch squares and add it to the pressure cooker with the bay leaves.

4. **Meanwhile,** heat the oil in a nonstick skillet. Sauté the onion for 5 minutes. Move the onion to one side of the skillet and add a few more drops of oil to the cleared space. Add the leeks. Sauté until soft, about 5 minutes, then add them to the pressure cooker. Add the bay leaves.

5. Lock the lid in place. Bring up to full pressure over high heat. Place a flame tamer under the pressure cooker and reduce the heat. Maintain high pressure for 6 minutes.

6. Quick-release the pressure. If the beans are not tender, simmer until they are, then add the salt.

7. Close the lid and let stand for 10 minutes, off the heat. Place a small amount of the hot soup in a small bowl, add the miso, whisk until smooth and return it to the pot. Stir and serve garnished with carrots.

adzuki chestnut soup

8-10 servings

This mahogany-colored soup is fabulous in the fall. Pressure-cooking reduces cooking time and quickly marries the flavor. It's delicious served with Homemade Sesame-Rice Crackers, *page 142.*

ingredients

1 cup dried, peeled chestnuts
5 cups water
2 cups dried adzuki beans
1 6-inch piece kombu
1 large onion, 1/3-inch pieces

2 large carrots, 1/2-inch pieces
1/4 tsp. ground cardamom
2 tsp. unrefined sea salt
1 sprinkle of grated nutmeg,
  optional (freshly grated is divine)

directions

1. Add the chestnuts and 5 cups of water to a pressure cooker. Let soak for about 6 hours. Pick over the adzuki beans to remove debris and broken beans. Wash the beans and place them in a large bowl. Cover them with water 2 inches above the level of beans and soak for 6 hours.

2. Cover the kombu with water and let soak for 5 minutes. Cut it into 1/2-inch squares and set aside.

3. Remove the chestnuts from the pressure cooker with a slotted spoon. Cut them in half. Pick out and discard any remaining chestnut skin. Return the chestnuts to the pressure cooker and bring to a boil.

4. Add the rinsed adzuki beans, kombu, onion, carrots and cardamom to the pressure cooker. Lock the lid in place. Bring up to full pressure over high heat. Place a flame tamer under the pressure cooker and reduce the heat. Maintain high pressure for 20 minutes.

5. Quick release the pressure. If the beans are not tender, simmer until they are, then add the salt.

6. Close the lid and let stand for 5 minutes, off the heat.

7. Transfer 5 cups of the soup to a blender and process until smooth. Return the purée to the pressure cooker. Serve garnished with a light sprinkling of nutmeg.

little red bean soup

10 servings

Little Red Bean Soup *makes a fortifying lunch or supper. This is because like most beans they are so rich in protein and iron. Red beans are related to kidney and pinto beans and can be substituted for them. They are used extensively in southern cooking.*

ingredients

2 cups dried red beans	2 tsp. ground cumin
1/2 tsp. canola oil	1 tsp. dried, ground oregano
2 onions, diced small	1 bay leaf
4 garlic cloves, minced	1 tsp. unrefined sea salt
7 cups water	3 TBS. barley miso
1 6-inch strip kombu	1 TBS. fresh parsley, minced, to
2 carrots, cut into 1/2-inch, 1/2 rounds	garnish

directions

1. The day before, pick over the red beans to remove debris and broken beans. Wash the beans and place them in a large bowl. Cover them with water, 2 inches above the level of the beans and soak overnight.

2. Heat the oil in a large, nonstick skillet. Sauté the onions until translucent, about 5 minutes. Add the garlic. Sauté for 1 minute, stirring constantly, then set aside.

3. Bring 7 cups of water to a boil in a pressure cooker. Add the rinsed beans and return to a boil. Simmer uncovered for 5 minutes, skimming off foam from the surface until it subsides.

4. **Meanwhile,** cover the kombu with water and let soak for 5 minutes. Cut it into 1/2-inch squares and add it to the pressure cooker. Add the onions, garlic, carrots, cumin, oregano and bay leaf to the pressure cooker.

5. Lock the lid in place. Bring up to high pressure over high heat. Place a flame tamer under the pressure cooker and reduce the heat. Maintain high pressure for 12 minutes.

6. Remove the pressure cooker from the heat and allow the pressure to come down naturally for 10 minutes. Quick-release the remaining pressure by placing the pressure cooker under cool, running water.

7. If the beans are not tender, simmer until they are, then add the salt.

8. Close the lid and let stand for 10 minutes, off the heat.

9. Place a small amount of the hot soup in a small bowl, add the miso, whisk until smooth and return it to the pressure cooker. Stir and served garnished with parsley.

variations
- Rather then pressure-cooking, simmer in a stock pot, with the lid ajar, for about 1 1/2 hours.
- For faster preparation, do not sauté the onion. Omit the oil.
- For a creamy consistency, blend 3 cups of the soup in step #9.

cook's tip
- Red beans are available at well-stocked grocery stores and at natural food stores.

mesquite split pea soup

10 servings

Enjoy the smoky flavor of mesquite grilling in this divine soup. The combination of spices and Liquid Smoke® is the secret to this southwest version of the classic pea soup. Serve with Indian Corn Muffins, *page 132.*

ingredients

2 cups green split peas
1 tsp. canola oil
1 medium onion, diced small
1 large carrot, 1/4-inch rounds
1 stalk celery, diced small
2 garlic cloves, minced
1 tsp. fennel seeds, crushed
6 1/2 cups boiling water
1 6-inch strip kombu

1 bay leaf
1/4 tsp. ground coriander
1/8 tsp. ground cloves
4 whole cloves
1 tsp. Liquid Smoke®
1 tsp. unrefined sea salt
1/8 tsp. white pepper
2 TBS. barley miso

directions

1. Pick over the split peas to remove debris and set aside.

2. Heat the oil in a pressure cooker and sauté the onion until translucent, about 5 minutes. Move the onion to one side of the pressure cooker and add a few more drops of oil to the cleared space. Add the carrot and sauté for several minutes. Repeat with the celery. Repeat with the garlic and fennel seeds, sautéing them together for 1 minute.

3. Add the rinsed peas and 6 1/2 cups of boiling water to the pressure cooker. Simmer uncovered for 5 minutes, skimming off foam from the surface until it subsides.

4. **Meanwhile,** cover the kombu with water and let soak for 5 minutes. Cut it into 1/2-inch squares and add it to the pressure cooker Add the bay leaf, coriander, cloves and Liquid Smoke® to the pressure cooker.

5. Lock the lid in place. Bring up to full pressure over high heat. Place a flame tamer under the pressure cooker and reduce the heat. Maintain high pressure for 25 minutes.

6. Quick-release the pressure. Add the salt and pepper. Close the lid and let stand for 10 minutes, off the heat.

7. Place a small amount of the hot soup in a small bowl, add the miso, whisk until smooth and return it to the pot. Stir and serve piping hot.

amazing adzuki soup

6 servings

This velvety combination of puréed adzuki beans and vegetables is a feast for the eyes. Fresh ginger root adds a sublime aroma. Serve with Nutty Spice Muffins, *page 135.*

ingredients

1 cup dried adzuki beans
4 cups water
1 6-inch strip kombu
1 medium carrot, into large pieces
1 onion, into large pieces

1/4 cup shoyu, or to taste
1 tsp. grated fresh ginger, juiced, page 46
1 TBS. scallion, thinly sliced, to garnish

directions

1. Pick over the adzuki beans to remove debris and broken beans. Wash the beans and set aside.

2. Add 4 cups of water to a pressure cooker and bring to a boil. Add the rinsed beans and return to a boil. Simmer uncovered for about 5 minutes, skimming off foam from the surface until it subsides.

3. **Meanwhile,** cover the kombu with water and let soak for 5 minutes. Cut it into 1/2-inch squares and add it to the pressure cooker. Add the carrot and onion to the pressure cooker.

4. Lock the lid in place. Bring up to full pressure over high heat. Place a flame tamer under the pressure cooker and reduce the heat. Maintain high pressure for 5 minutes.

5. Quick-release the pressure. If the beans are not tender, simmer until they are, then add the shoyu and ginger juice.

6. Transfer 3 cups of soup to a blender and process until smooth. Return the purée to the pressure cooker and stir. Serve garnished with scallions.

variations

- For express adzuki soup, substitute canned beans. Rinse the beans and add them in step #6.
- I prefer to soak the beans overnight for a more digestible soup.

notes

express soups

In a hurry? This chapter is for you! All of these recipes can be prepared in less than an hour from start to finish. In addition, most leftover soups can be blended and used as an instant sauce over rice or noodles later in the week.

Here are my favorite techniques to speed preparation. I frequently use a pressure cooker because it dramatically reduces cooking time. To get a head start on cooking, I begin to boil water before gathering the ingredients for the recipe. Lastly, I use fast-cooking beans like lentils or split peas and organic canned beans. Natural food stores now sell organic canned beans, cooked with kombu, making them more digestible. They are as low in calories and sodium as homecooked beans.

Save time by keeping a few, basic food staples on hand. You can make almost every recipe in this chapter without ever going to the store. Foods to have on-hand include dried and canned beans, kombu sea vegetable, onions, garlic, carrots, celery, fresh gingerroot and barley miso.

See "All About Beans" for helpful information about their preparation, page 15.

southwestern black-eyed pea soup

4 servings

This soup is great as a side dish with wholesome bread, steamed vegetables or a salad. It also doubles as a luscious filling for a Mexican-style burrito.

ingredients

1 cup dried black-eyed peas
3 cups water
1 6-inch strip kombu

1/2 tsp. ground cumin
3/4 tsp. mild chili powder
2 TBS. shoyu, or more to taste

directions

1. Pick over the black-eyed peas to remove debris and broken peas. Set aside.

2. Bring 3 cups of water to a boil in a pressure cooker. Add the rinsed peas and return to a boil. Simmer, uncovered, for 5 minutes, skimming off foam from the surface until it subsides.

3. **Meanwhile,** cover the kombu with water and let soak for 5 minutes. Cut it into 1/2-inch squares and add it to the pressure cooker. Add the cumin and chili powder to the pressure cooker.

4. Lock the lid in place. Bring up to full pressure over high heat. Place a flame tamer under the pressure cooker and reduce the heat. Maintain high pressure for 8 minutes.

5. Quick-release the pressure. If the peas are not soft, simmer until they are, then add the shoyu.

crushed yellow split pea soup

12 servings

The classic tastes of India are reflected in this soothing soup. The split peas melt-in-your mouth, making this a great comfort food. Inspired by a recipe from Didi Emmons' Vegetarian Planet.

ingredients

2 1/2 cups yellow split peas
1 6-inch strip kombu
1 tsp. canola oil
1 medium onion, diced small
4 garlic cloves, minced
2 medium carrots, cut into rounds

8 cups boiling water
1/2 tsp. dried tarragon
1/4 tsp. dried thyme
1 TBS. unrefined sea salt
1/4 cup sweet, white miso, puréed in 1/2 cup water

directions

1. Pick over the split peas for debris and set aside.

2. Cover the kombu with water and let soak for 5 minutes. Cut it into 1/2-inch squares and set aside.

3. Heat the oil in a pressure cooker. Add the onion and sauté over low heat until soft, about 5 minutes. Add the garlic and stir constantly for 1 minute.

4. Add the carrots, boiling water, tarragon, thyme and kombu. Rinse the split peas and add to the pressure cooker.

5. Lock the lid in place. Bring up to full pressure over high heat. Place a flame tamer under the pressure cooker and reduce the heat. Maintain high pressure for 15 minutes.

6. Quick-release the pressure. If the peas are not soft, simmer until they are, then add the salt.

7. Close the lid and let stand for 5 minutes, off the heat.

8. Place a small amount of the hot soup in a small bowl, add the miso, whisk until smooth and return it to the pressure cooker.

express chestnut lentil soup

10 servings

Chestnuts are not just for holidays anymore! Along with cardamom, cinnamon and carrots, they add a sweet dimension to this gourmet lentil soup. Although it's faster to use canned chestnuts, I enjoy the experience of cooking with dried ones.

ingredients

1 6-inch strip kombu
1 1/2 cups brown lentils
5 cups boiling water
2 large carrots, cut into 1/2-inch sliced diagonals

1 medium onion, diced medium
1/2 tsp. ground cinnamon
1/4 tsp. ground cardamom, optional
1 7-ounce jar cooked chestnuts
1 1/2 tsp. unrefined sea salt

directions

1. Cover the kombu with water and let soak for 5 minutes. Cut it into 1/2-inch squares and add it to a pressure cooker.

2. **Meanwhile,** pick over the lentils to remove debris. Add the rinsed lentils to the pressure cooker. Add the remaining ingredients, except the cooked chestnuts and salt.

3. Lock the lid in place. Bring up to full pressure over high heat. Place a flame tamer under the pressure cooker and reduce the heat. Maintain high pressure for 7 minutes.

4. Remove the pressure cooker from the heat and allow the pressure to come down naturally for 15 minutes. Then, quick-release the remaining pressure. Add the cooked chestnuts.

5. If the lentils are not soft, simmer until they are, then add the salt. Close the lid and let stand for 5 minutes, off the heat.

variation

• Soak 1/2 cup dried chestnuts with 3 cups of water for 8 hours. With a slotted spoon, remove red skin that has floated to the top and take the chestnuts out of the soaking water. Remove any skin still clinging to the chestnuts. Cut the chestnuts in half and return to the pressure cooker. Proceed to step #1.

curried split pea soup

This soup is a welcome antidote for the winter blues. Cumin, fennel and black mustard are the three robust seeds that transform split peas into a curried delight which will wake up your taste buds.

ingredients

2 cups green split peas
1 6-inch strip kombu
2 tsp. sesame oil
1 tsp. whole cumin seeds
1/2 tsp. fennel seeds
1 tsp. black mustard seeds
1 large onion, diced small
1 TBS. fresh ginger, peeled and minced

1 tsp. minced garlic
3 large carrots, cut into 1/4-inch rounds
6 cups boiling water
2 TBS. mild curry powder
1 TBS. unrefined sea salt, or more to taste

directions

1. Pick over the peas for debris and set aside. Cover the kombu with water and let soak for 5 minutes. Cut it into 1/2-inch squares and set aside.

2. Heat the oil in a pressure cooker and add the cumin, fennel and mustard seeds. Sauté until they sizzle and pop, 5 - 10 seconds. Add the onion, ginger and garlic. Stir constantly for 1 minute.

3. Add the rinsed peas, carrots, boiling water, curry powder and kombu to the pressure cooker. Lock the lid in place. Bring up to full pressure over high heat. Place a flame tamer under the pressure cooker and reduce the heat. Maintain high pressure for 20 minutes.

4. Quick-release the pressure. If the beans are not tender, simmer until they are, then add the salt. Close the lid and let stand for 5 minutes, off the heat.

cook's tip

- For the best curry flavor, use *Lorna's Curry Powder*, page 146

spicy red bean soup

8 servings

Mild chiles, oregano and garlic transform these little red beans into a south-of-the-border sensation. If you really want to turn up the heat, substitute jalapeño chiles for the Anaheim chiles. Serve with Muffins Mexicana, *page 131.*

ingredients

2 cups dried red beans
1 6-inch strip kombu
3 6-inch Anaheim (mild) chiles
6 cups boiling water
1 large onion, diced small

3 garlic cloves, minced
1 tsp. dried, ground oregano
2 tsp. unrefined sea salt
1 1/2 TBS. shoyu

directions

1. Pick over the red beans to remove debris and broken beans. Wash the beans and place them in a medium pot. Use the "speedy soak" method, page 16.

2. Cover the kombu with water and let soak for 5 minutes. Cut it into 1/2-inch squares and set aside.

3. Remove the seeds from the chiles, then cut them into 2-inch sections.

4. **Meanwhile,** bring 6 cups of water to a boil in a pressure cooker. Add the rinsed beans and return to a boil. Simmer uncovered for 5 minutes, skimming the foam from the surface until it subsides.

5. Add the kombu, chiles, onion, garlic and oregano to the pressure cooker. Lock the lid in place. Bring up to full pressure over high heat. Place a flame tamer under the pressure cooker and reduce the heat. Maintain high pressure for 12 minutes.

6. Quick-release the pressure. If the beans are not tender, simmer until they are. Then add the salt and shoyu.

7. Close the lid and let stand for 5 minutes, off the heat. Add more shoyu to taste.

variations

- Substitute two 2-inch jalapeño peppers for the Anaheim chiles.
- Substitute kidney beans for the red beans.
- For a creamier consistency, cut the chiles into large pieces and add them to a blender with 4 cups of the soup. Process until uniform in color and return to the pot.

dilled broccoli soup

10 servings

Dill adds a distinct undertone to this velvety broccoli soup. Since it is pressure-cooked, you will have it on your table in about twenty minutes. Another recipe adapted from the outstanding cookbook, Lorna Sass' Complete Vegetarian Kitchen.

ingredients

4 cups water
1 large bunch broccoli
1/2 tsp. Herbamare®
1 jumbo onion, cut into large pieces

1/3 cup rolled oats
2 TBS. sweet, white miso
1/4 cup fresh dill, tightly packed
1 fresh dill sprig per serving, to garnish

directions

1. Bring 4 cups of water to a boil in a pressure cooker. **Meanwhile,** separate the broccoli into florets. Peel the broccoli stalks and cut them into large pieces. Add all of the broccoli, the Herbamere®, onion and oats to the pressure cooker

2. Lock the lid in place. Bring up to full pressure over high heat. Place a flame tamer under the pressure cooker and reduce the heat. Maintain high pressure for 5 minutes.

3. Quick-release the pressure under cool, running water.

4. Transfer the soup to a blender with the miso and the dill. Process until smooth. Serve in individual soup bowls, each garnished with a fresh dill sprig.

variation

- Rather than pressure-cooking, simmer in a stock pot for 20 minutes.

speedy green split pea soup

8 servings

Would you believe split pea soup in thirty minutes? Warming and tasty, this soup is sure to become a favorite. Serve with sourdough bread and a salad.

ingredients

2 cups green split peas
1 6-inch strip kombu
1 tsp. canola oil
2 medium onions, diced small
2 garlic cloves, minced
1/2 tsp. dried thyme
1 bay leaf

2 TBS. pearled barley
2 carrots, cut into 1/4-inch rounds
6 1/2 cups boiling water
1 tsp. unrefined sea salt
2 TBS. barley miso, puréed in 1/4 cup water

directions

1. Pick over the split peas to remove debris and set aside.

2. Cover the kombu with water and let soak for 5 minutes. Cut it into 1/2-inch squares and set aside.

3. Heat the oil in a pressure cooker. Over low heat, sauté the onions until translucent, about 5 minutes. Add the garlic and thyme. Stir constantly for 1 minute.

4. Add the rinsed peas, kombu, bay leaf, barley, carrots and boiling water to the pressure cooker.

5. Lock the lid in place. Bring up to full pressure over high heat. Place a flame tamer under the pot and reduce the heat. Maintain high pressure for 15 minutes.

6. Quick-release the pressure. If the peas are not soft, simmer until they are, then add the salt. Close the lid and let stand for 5 minutes, off the heat.

7. Place a small amount of the hot soup in a small bowl, add the miso, whisk until smooth and return it to the pressure cooker.

variations
- Substitute Job's tears for pearled barley.
- To reduce the cooking time, do not sauté the onions, garlic and thyme. Simply add them to pressure cooker in step #4.

cook's tip
- Rinse legumes such as split peas and lentils just before cooking. This prevents them from sticking to the strainer.

yellow split pea and barley soup

12 servings

The ingredients in this soup are almost always on hand, so it can be a last-minute meal-saver. The creamy texture and hint of herbs will win you over. Serve with Moist and Hearty Oatmeal Muffins, *page 137.*

ingredients

2 cups yellow split peas	1 large carrot, matchsticks
1 6-inch strip kombu	1/2 tsp. dried marjoram
1/2 tsp. sesame oil	1/4 tsp. dried rosemary
1 large onion, diced	1 bay leaf
3 garlic cloves, minced	2 tsp. unrefined sea salt
2 TBS. pearled barley	1 TBS. barley miso
7 cups boiling water	1 TBS. sweet, white miso

directions

1. Pick over the split peas to remove debris and set aside. Cover the kombu with water and let soak for 5 minutes. Cut the kombu into 1/2-inch squares and set aside.

2. **Meanwhile,** heat the oil in a pressure cooker. Sauté the onion for 3 minutes. Move the onion to one side of the pressure cooker and add a few more drops of oil to the cleared space. Add the minced garlic. Sauté for 1 minute, stirring constantly.

3. Add the rinsed peas and pearled barley to the pressure cooker. Add 7 cups of boiling water, the carrots, marjoram, rosemary and bay leaf. Lock the lid in place. Over high heat, bring up to full pressure. Place a flame tamer under the pressure cooker and reduce the heat. Maintain high pressure for 20 minutes.

4. Quick-release the pressure. If the peas are not soft, simmer until they are, then add the salt.

5. Close the lid and let stand for 5 minutes, off the heat.

6. Place a small amount of the hot soup in a small bowl, add the miso, whisk until smooth and return it to the pressure cooker. Adjust the flavor by adding more miso.

variation

*   Substitute green split peas or red lentils for the yellow split peas.

notes

quick breads and spreads

The aroma of homemade muffins, cornbread and other quick breads fresh from the oven, creates an ambiance of love and caring. They can be prepared in less than an hour and freeze well. You can make soup and baked goods and eat them together throughout the week.

You will discover a delightful taste difference when you use wholesome ingredients such as whole wheat pastry flour, canola oil, maple syrup and brown rice syrup. This is in contrast with commercial baked goods, which are made with overprocessed white flour, so-called flavor enhancers, and high quantities of saturated fat and refined sugar. Rather than tasting intensely sweet and oily, homemade quick breads are hearty, deliciously moist and low in fat. Feel free to indulge.

My approach to quick breads is to combine the dry ingredients and the wet ingredients separately. First, use a blender or a whisk to thoroughly mix the wet ingredients, including the salt. Before pouring sticky syrups into measuring cups and spoons, brush them with oil. Syrups will glide out more easily this way. Next, use a whisk to evenly combine the dry ingredients. This ensures that the baking powder is evenly distributed and also eliminates the sifting step.

Now, briefly whisk the wet ingredients and the dry ingredients together just until the flour is absorbed. Although some small lumps may remain, they will disappear during baking. Avoid overmixing because it will result in heavy baked goods. A whisk combines dry and wet ingredients more quickly and gently than a spoon.

What to spread on bread? It's best to avoid saturated or hydrogenated fats like butter and margarine. Solid at room temperature, they clog the arteries. Instead, use an unsaturated, non-hydrogenated spread like Spectrum Naturals®. It is made of canola oil and even tastes like butter! Buy it at your local natural food store. Otherwise, you can make any of the spreads in this chapter in less than ten minutes. They offer protein, great flavor and little or no fat. Lastly, for a fat-free bread topping, use natural fruit preserves.

cook's tips

- Arrowroot powder can be substituted for egg replacer in any recipe, in equal amounts.
- If the batter is too wet, add one tablespoon of flour at a time. If too dry, gradually add one tablespoon of water.
- I prefer to use coarsely chopped nuts rather than crushed.
- Use a spring-action ice cream scoop to make uniform muffins fast.
- Using individual paper muffin cups is a sticky proposition. Because the batter sticks to the paper, I do not use them. Rather, I brush the muffin tins with oil.
- After baking, allow the muffins to stand in the tins for 5 minutes. Then use a large spoon to guide them out.
- Place muffins on a rack to cool completely before freezing. I freeze them in wide-mouth glass canning jars. To thaw, set on the counter for 10 minutes or warm in a steamer for 2 minutes.

zesty white bean spread

1 1/2 cups

Smooth this robust spread over a slice of crusty, sourdough bread to complement a simple vegetable soup for lunch.

ingredients

1 15-ounce can white beans, drained and rinsed	1 TBS. sweet, white miso
2 tsp. fresh lemon juice	1/4 tsp. dried marjoram
1 tsp. capers, optional	1/2 tsp. dried basil
1 tsp. extra-virgin olive oil	1/2 tsp. dried thyme
1/2 tsp. dried, ground oregano	1/8 tsp. white pepper
	2-3 TBS. water

directions

1. Combine all the ingredients in a food processor or blender. Process until uniform in color, adding water as needed.

2. Transfer to a small pot and simmer to meld flavors, about 5 minutes. Serve hot or cold.

variations
- Substitute homecooked beans for canned beans.
- For a coarse purée, mash with a fork instead of using a food processor or blender.

almond spread

1 cup

Try this spread as a low-fat alternative to peanut butter. It is rich in beta carotene and yummy too!

ingredients

1/2 cup water
2 cups carrots, coarsely cut
1/4 tsp. unrefined sea salt

2 TBS. almond butter
1 1/2 tsp. shoyu

directions

1. Bring the water to a boil in a small pot. Add the carrots and salt. Simmer for 10 minutes.

2. Drain, reserving the cooking water.

3. Add all of the ingredients to a blender and process until uniform in color. Add more water, as needed, to reach a spreadable consistency.

variation

• Substitute any nut or seed butter for the almond butter.

sunflower spread

2 1/2 cups

Here is a tasty spread made without the saturated fat and cholesterol of butter. The tofu and tahini contribute protein and calcium. Umeboshi vinegar's salty-sour taste adds instant pizzazz.

ingredients

1 pound soft tofu	2 TBS. brown rice syrup
1/2 cup sunflower seeds, toasted and chopped	3 TBS. sweet, white miso
	1 TBS. tahini
3 TBS. umeboshi vinegar	1/4-1/2 cup water

directions

1. Steam the tofu for 5 minutes, then place it in a food processor, fitted with a metal blade, or a suribachi. Add the remaining ingredients. Purée, adding water to achieve the desired consistency.

variations

- Substitute lemon juice for the umeboshi vinegar.
- Add 3 tablespoons of minced, raw or blanched onion.

golden sweet spread

1 cup

This guilt-free spread will satisfy your sweet craving like no jelly can. Next time you bake yams for dinner, add an extra one to the oven for a head start on this recipe.

ingredients

1 small garnet yam
1 small garlic clove
1/8 tsp. extra virgin olive oil
1 tsp. fresh lemon juice
1/8 tsp. ground oregano

1 pinch unrefined sea salt
1 dash white pepper, optional
2 TBS. tahini
2 tsp. fresh parsley, minced

directions

1. Preheat the oven to 400°F. Wash the yam and pierce with a fork in several places. Place in a baking dish and bake until very soft, about an hour.

2. **Meanwhile,** slice 1/8 inch off the top of a bulb of garlic. Drizzle olive oil over the exposed top of the garlic bulb. Place the garlic bulb in a covered baking dish. Bake until soft and golden, about 30 minutes. Set aside to cool.

3. Press one garlic clove out of its skin and place in a food processor, fitted with a metal blade. Slice open and scoop out the insides of the yam. Add it to the food processor. Add the lemon juice, oregano, salt, pepper, tahini and parsley. Process, adding water as needed, to make a creamy consistency.

4. Serve this spread with sourdough bread or with vegetables as a dip. It will keep refrigerated about a week.

hummus-in-a-hurry

3 cups

Looking for a party-pleaser or a quick meal? This high-calcium, easy spread can be served as a dip with rolled romaine lettuce leaves, pita bread or lavosh. For an instant lunch or dinner, stuff into whole wheat pita bread with shredded lettuce.

ingredients

2 large garlic cloves
2 stalks celery, coarsely chopped
1/2 cup fresh lemon juice
1 15-ounce can organic chickpeas
1/4 cup tahini
2 tsp. shoyu
1 pinch cayenne, optional
4 pepperocini, to garnish, optional

directions

1. Add the garlic, celery and lemon juice to a food processor, fitted with a metal blade. Process for 1 minute. Add the rinsed beans, tahini, shoyu and cayenne. Process until smooth and creamy.

2. Serve garnished with pepperocini.

variation

• Garnish with a sprinkle of extra-virgin olive oil and paprika.

cook's tip

• A food processor is the best choice for puréing hummus. A blender will do, but may require additional liquid, causing the spread to have a thinner consistency.

savory bagel spread
1 cup

This quick, savory, high-calcium spread is a memorable alternative to margarine or butter. High in protein and low in fat, it can be added to a salad instead of cheese. Kudos to Ron Roush, a gourmet cook, who suggested the addition of brown rice syrup and using silken tofu instead of soft tofu. He loves this spread as a substitute for cream cheese on a bagel.

ingredients
- 1/2 pound soft tofu
- 1 TBS. tahini, or more to taste
- 2 TBS. barley miso, or more to taste
- 1/2 tsp. brown rice syrup, optional

directions
1. Steam the tofu for 4 minutes. Crumble it into a food processor, fitted with a metal blade. Add the tahini and miso and mix well. Add a few tablespoons of water, as needed, to reach a creamy consistency.

2. Store in a glass jar in the refrigerator. It keeps about a week.

variations
- Add a pinch of dried oregano, basil, thyme or dill in step #1.
- Substitute a box of firm silken tofu for the soft tofu and do not steam it.
- Add 1/2 teaspoon of brown rice syrup in step #1.

cook's tip
- To store the extra 1/2 pound of tofu, leave it in the container covered with fresh water. Change the water every other day. It will keep for one week.

southern style biscuits

18 biscuits

I wanted to create healthy southern-style biscuits without the butter or white flour. After some experimentation, this recipe was born. Serve with Traditional Navy Bean Soup, *page 102.*

wet ingredients

1/4 cup boiling water
1 1/2 tsp. unrefined sea salt
1 cup water
1/2 cup unrefined corn oil
1 1/4 cups EdenBlend® beverage

dry ingredients

7 cups whole wheat pastry flour
1 TBS. Rumford® baking powder

directions

1. Dissolve the salt in 1/4 cup of boiling water. Add 1 cup of water to cool it and set aside.

2. Preheat the oven to 450°F. Brush a cookie sheet with oil and set aside.

3. Combine the dry ingredients in a bowl and mix well. Cut the oil into the flour with a fork or pastry blender. Form a well in the center of the mixture. Pour the salt water and the EdenBlend® beverage into the well. Mix the dough with your hands until it holds together in a ball. The consistency should be that of a moist pie crust dough.

4. Roll out the dough to a 3/4-inch thickness between 2 sheets of wax paper. Cut out 3-inch circles with a biscuit cutter or glass rim.

5. Arrange the biscuits on the cookie sheet so that their edges touch each other. Bake until golden brown on the bottom, 12 - 15 minutes.

variations
- Add 2 tablespoons of chopped chives in step #2.
- To make "buttermilk" biscuits, add 2-3 tablespoons of lemon juice in step #2.

sweet cornbread

Cornbread is the classic companion to spicy soups, chilies and stews. Try it with Fabulous Chipotle Baked Beans, page 85, or Spicy Black Bean Chili, page 81.

wet ingredients

1/4 cup canola oil
3/4-1 cup EdenBlend® beverage
2 TBS. brown rice syrup
2 TBS. maple syrup
1 TBS. natural vanilla
1/2 tsp. unrefined sea salt

dry ingredients

1 1/2 cups whole wheat pastry flour
1/2 cups fine-ground cornmeal
4 tsp. Rumford® baking powder

directions

1. Preheat the oven to 350°F. Brush an 8-inch baking pan with oil and set aside.

2. Combine the wet ingredients in a blender and process until uniform in color.

3. Combine the dry ingredients in a bowl and mix well with a whisk.

4. Pour the wet mixture into the dry mixture and briefly blend with a whisk. Pour the batter into the baking pan. Bake uncovered until a toothpick inserted in the middle comes out dry and the cornbread is golden brown, about 25 minutes.

5. Let stand 5 - 10 minutes before serving.

macrobiotic cornbread

6-8 servings

This cornbread is heavier and more wholesome than typical sweet cornbreads because it is made with cooked brown rice. I love to eat it with Macro Baked Beans, *page 86, or for a satisfying guilt-free snack.*

ingredients

3 cups coarse cornmeal
1 cup whole wheat pastry flour
2 TBS. Rumford® baking powder
2 1/2 cups cooked brown rice
3 TBS. unrefined corn oil

1 3/4 cups hot water
1 tsp. unrefined sea salt
1 TBS. black sesame seeds, to garnish

directions

1. Preheat the oven to 350°F. Brush an 8-inch square baking pan with oil and set aside.

2. Mix the cornmeal, flour and baking powder thoroughly in a bowl. Add the cooked rice, breaking up any lumps with your hands. Mix well.

3. Whisk together the oil, hot water and salt in a measuring cup. Pour it into the dry mixture and mix gently. Let stand for 5 minutes to absorb the liquid until thick and "squishy." Add more water if needed.

4. Press the dough into the baking pan. Smooth out the top with wet hands and sprinkle the sesame seeds on top. Bake, covered, for 30 minutes.

5. Remove the cover and bake until the testing wire comes out dry, 20 - 30 minutes. Cool before slicing.

variations

• Add one 4-ounce can of diced green chiles in step #3.
• Add 1 cup of corn kernels in step #3.

muffins mexicana

12 muffins

These festive cornmeal muffins are the perfect accompaniment to any Mexican soup. You can "kick them up a notch" by adding specks of diced of green chiles.

wet ingredients

2 TBS. unrefined corn oil
1 cup red bell pepper, minced
1 1/2 cups water
1/2 tsp. unrefined sea salt

dry ingredients

1 1/2 cups whole wheat pastry flour
1 1/4 cups cornmeal
1 TBS. Rumford® baking powder
1 TBS. EnerG® egg replacer

directions

1. Heat the oil in a small, nonstick skillet. Sauté the red pepper until soft, about 8 minutes.

2. **Meanwhile,** preheat the oven to 400°F. Brush two 6-hole muffin tins with oil and set aside.

3. Add the wet ingredients to a blender and process until uniform in color.

4. Combine the dry ingredients in a bowl and mix well. Pour the wet ingredients into the dry mixture and briefly blend with a whisk. Add the red pepper.

5. Fill the muffin tins to the top. Bake until golden brown and a toothpick inserted in the middle comes out dry, 15 - 20 minutes.

6. Allow the muffins to cool for 10 minutes in the tins before removing to a wire rack.

variations

- Substitute arrowroot powder for the egg replacer.
- Add 1/4 cup of diced green chiles in step #4.
- Substitute 1 cup of corn or diced yellow summer squash or zucchini for the red bell pepper.

indian corn muffins

12 muffins

These muffins are reminiscent of the sweetness of Indian Summer. They go well with a spicy or savory soup like Mesquite Split Pea Soup, *page 106.*

wet ingredients

1/4 cup unrefined corn oil
3 TBS. brown rice syrup
3 TBS. maple syrup
1 1/2 cups water
1 1/2 tsp. brown rice vinegar
1/2 tsp. unrefined sea salt

dry ingredients

2 1/4 cups cornmeal
1 1/2 cups whole wheat pastry flour
1 1/2 TBS. Rumford® baking powder

directions

1. Preheat the oven to 400°F. Brush two 6-hole muffin tins with oil and set aside.

2. Combine the wet ingredients in a blender and process until uniform in color.

3. Combine the dry ingredients in a bowl and mix well. Pour the wet mixture into the dry mixture and briefly blend with a whisk.

4. Fill the muffin tins 3/4 full with the batter. Bake until golden brown and a toothpick inserted in the middle comes out dry, 20 - 25 minutes.

5. Allow the muffins to cool for 10 minutes in the tins before removing to a wire rack.

variations

- Add 1/2 cup toasted sunflower seeds in step #3.
- For *Cranberry Orange Muffins,* substitute 1 1/2 cups of orange juice for the water and add 1/2 cup chopped fresh cranberries in step #3.

herbal corn muffins

10-12 muffins

These herb-infused muffins make a wonderful addition to soup, chili or stew. They are particularly tasty with Broccoli Squash Purée, *page 29, and* Creamy Baked Anasazi Beans, *page 80.*

wet ingredients

3 TBS. unrefined corn oil
2 TBS. brown rice syrup
1 1⁄4 cups water
1⁄4 tsp. unrefined sea salt

dry ingredients

1 1⁄2 cups whole wheat pastry flour
1 1⁄2 cups cornmeal
1 tsp. dried sage
3 TBS. fresh dill, minced
1 TBS. Rumford® baking powder
2 TBS. egg replacer
2 TBS. poppy seeds

directions

1. Preheat the oven to 400°F. Brush two 6-hole muffin tins with oil and set aside.

2. Combine the wet ingredients in a blender and process until uniform in color.

3. Mix all of the dry ingredients, except the poppy seeds, in a bowl. Pour the wet mixture into the dry mixture and briefly mix with a whisk.

4. Fill the muffin tins 3⁄4 full with the batter and top with the poppy seeds. Bake until golden brown and a toothpick inserted in the middle comes out dry, 15 - 20 minutes.

5. Allow the muffins to cool for 10 minutes in the tins before removing to a wire rack.

variations

- Substitute sesame seeds for the poppy seeds.
- Add 1 ear of corn, off the cob, in step #3.
- Substitute 1 tablespoon of dried dill for the fresh dill.

double corn muffins

12 muffins

These versatile muffins are great for breakfast, a snack or to accompany any meal. They are especially good with organic canned beans, if you're in a hurry.

wet ingredients

- 3 TBS. unrefined corn oil
- 2 TBS. brown rice syrup
- 2 TBS. maple syrup
- 1 tsp. brown rice vinegar
- 1 cup water
- 1/2 tsp. unrefined sea salt

dry ingredients

- 1 1/2 cups cornmeal
- 1 1/2 cups whole wheat pastry flour
- 1 TBS. Rumford® baking powder
- 2 ears of corn, cut kernels off the cob

directions

1. Preheat the oven to 400°F. Brush two 6-hole muffin tins with oil and set aside.

2. Combine the wet ingredients in a blender and process until uniform in color.

3. Combine the dry ingredients, except the corn kernels, in a bowl. Mix well with a whisk.

4. Pour the wet mixture into the dry mixture and briefly blend with a whisk. Gradually add water, as needed, to make a loose batter. Gently stir in the corn kernels.

5. Fill the muffin tins to the top. Bake until golden brown and a toothpick inserted in the middle comes out dry, 20 - 25 minutes.

6. Allow the muffins to cool for 10 minutes in the tins before removing to a wire rack.

variation

- Add 1/3 cup diced, red bell peppers to step #4.

cook's tip

- Frozen organic corn kernels, packaged by Cascadian Farms,® are available year-round in natural food stores. Substitute one cup frozen for two ears of corn.

nutty spice muffins

10-12 muffins

The enticing aroma of spices and fresh lemon fill the kitchen as these muffins bake. You won't find a better muffin in any coffee shop. Serve with Amazing Adzuki Soup, *page 107.*

wet ingredients

- 3 TBS. sesame oil
- 3 TBS. maple syrup
- 2 TBS. brown rice syrup
- 3⁄4 cup water
- 2 TBS. fresh lemon juice
- 1 TBS. lemon rind, grated
- 2 small yellow squash, grated
- 1⁄4 tsp. unrefined sea salt

dry ingredients

- 1 3⁄4 cups whole wheat pastry flour
- 1⁄4 cup oat bran
- 1 tsp. cinnamon
- 1⁄4 tsp. ground ginger
- 2 TBS. egg replacer
- 1 TBS. Rumford® baking powder
- 1⁄2 cup pecans, toasted and chopped
- 2 TBS. sunflower seeds

directions

1. Preheat the oven to 400°F. Brush two 6-hole muffin tins with oil and set aside.

2. Combine the wet ingredients in a blender. Process until the mixture becomes uniform in color and then set aside.

3. Add the squash to a food processor that is fitted with a metal blade. Add the dry ingredients, except the pecans and sunflower seeds. Process briefly, then transfer to a bowl.

4. Pour the wet mixture into the dry mixture and gently whisk together. Add the pecans. Add more water, as needed, to make a loose batter.

5. Fill the muffin tins 3⁄4 full with the batter. Top with the sunflower seeds. Bake until golden brown and a toothpick inserted in the middle comes out dry, 20 - 25 minutes.

6. Allow the muffins to cool for 10 minutes in the tins before removing to a wire rack.

secret sweet potato muffins

12 muffins

When you bite into this muffin, you will find an ambrosial treasure. Each muffin conceals a luscious, whipped yam filling. Reach for this gem the next time you crave a sweet snack. Make extra since they freeze well.

wet ingredients

- 1   medium garnet yam
- 2 TBS. corn oil
- 1/4 cup maple syrup
- 1/4 cup Sweet Cloud® brown rice syrup or barley malt syrup
- 2 cups water
- 1/4 tsp. unrefined sea salt

dry ingredients

- 3 cups whole wheat pastry flour
- 1 TBS. Rumford® baking powder
- 2 TBS. arrowroot powder
- 1/4 cup oat bran
- 3/4 cup pecans, toasted and chopped

directions

1. Preheat the oven 400°F. Brush two 6-hole muffin tins with oil and set aside.

2. Prick the yam with a fork in several places and place in a baking pan. Bake until very soft, about an hour. Allow to cool enough to handle. Scoop out the insides of the yam, mash and set aside.

3. **Meanwhile,** sift the flour, baking powder and arrowroot into a mixing bowl. Add the bran and the pecans.

4. Add the wet ingredients, except the yam, to a blender. Process until uniform in color.

5. Pour the wet mixture into the dry mixture and briefly blend with a whisk. Fill the oiled muffin tins half full.

6. Spoon a dab of mashed yam in the center of the muffin. Spoon enough batter over the yam to cover. Bake until a toothpick comes out dry, 45 - 60 minutes.

7. Allow muffins to cool 10 minutes in the tins before placing on a wire rack.

variations

- Substitute buttercup squash or canned pumpkin for the sweet potato.
- Add 1 teaspoon of pumpkin pie spices in step #3.
- Instead of using toasted and chopped pecans, place a pecan half on top of each muffin in step #6.

moist and hearty oatmeal muffins

9 muffins

These nutty and nutritious muffins freeze well and are a perfect on-the-run instant breakfast. Add a travel mug of Roma® or tea and you are set for the morning!

wet ingredients

1/4 cup canola oil
1/4 pound soft tofu
1 cup water
1/4 tsp. unrefined sea salt

dry ingredients

1 cup whole wheat pastry flour
2 cups rolled oats
1/2 cup sunflower seeds
1/2 tsp. cinnamon
1 TBS. Rumford® baking powder

directions

1. Preheat the oven to 375°F. Brush two 6-hole muffin tins with oil and set aside.

2. Combine the wet ingredients in a blender. Process until uniform in color and set aside.

3. Sift the flour through a single mesh strainer into a bowl. Combine the remaining dry ingredients in the bowl and mix well.

4. Pour the wet mixture into the dry mixture and briefly blend with a whisk.

5. Allow the batter to stand for 10 minutes to absorb the liquid. The desired texture is that of tuna salad. Add more water, if needed.

6. Fill the muffin tins to the top. Bake until the muffins are golden brown and a toothpick inserted in the middle comes out dry, 20 - 30 minutes.

7. Allow the muffins to cool for 10 minutes in the tins before removing to a wire rack.

variations

- Replace the tofu with 2/3 cup of water.
- To make these muffins moister, chewier and even more wholesome, add 1 cup leftover rice or other cooked grain and 1/4 cup of water to step #5.
- To sweeten the muffins, omit the tofu. Instead, add a combination of 1/4 cup brown rice syrup, 1/4 cup barley malt syrup, and reduce the water to 3/4 cup water. Or, use a combination of 1/4 cup brown rice syrup, 1/4 cup maple syrup, and 3/4 cup water. In addition, add 1/4 cup raisins or currants.

parsnip couscous muffins

10 muffins

Try these nutty, no-bake muffins the next time you are craving a quick snack. They are quick and guilt-free, so you can whip them up even on a weeknight.

wet ingredients

- 1 large parsnip, grated
- 2 cups pecan amazake
- 1 cup water
- 1/4 tsp. unrefined sea salt

dry ingredients

- 3/4 cup white couscous
- 3/4 cup brown couscous
- 1/2 cup pecans, toasted and chopped, optional

directions

1. Add the wet ingredients to a pot. Cover and simmer for 5 minutes.

2. **Meanwhile,** brush two 6-hole muffin tins with oil and set aside.

3. Add the white and brown couscous to the pot. Simmer, uncovered, until a porridge consistency is reached, about 8 minutes. Stir occasionally.

4. Gently stir in the pecans. Fill the muffin tins to the top, firmly pressing the mixture into the tins. Allow to solidify before serving, about an hour.

variations

- Substitute two large, grated carrots for the parsnip.
- Substitute almond amazake for the pecan amazake and toasted almonds for the pecans.
- Use 1 1/2 cups total white couscous instead of a mix of white and brown couscous.

wheat-free muffins

10 muffins

If you are on a wheat-free diet, it can be challenging to find a good muffin. These muffins pair rice flour and oat bran with natural sweeteners for a sensational alternative. Add the optional toasted sunflower seeds for a little crunch.

wet ingredients

- 1/4 cup unrefined corn oil
- 1/4 cup maple syrup
- 1/4 cup brown rice syrup
- 1 tsp. natural vanilla
- 1/4 tsp. unrefined sea salt
- 1/3 cup water
- 1/2 cup cooked brown rice, optional

dry ingredients

- 2 cups rice flour
- 1/4 cup oat bran
- 2 tsp. Rumford® baking powder
- 2 TBS. egg replacer

directions

1. Preheat the oven to 400°F. Brush two 6-hole muffin tins with oil and set aside.

2. Combine the wet ingredients, except the rice, in a blender. Process until the mixture becomes uniform in color. Add the rice and process for about 5 seconds.

3. Combine the dry ingredients in a bowl and mix well. Pour the wet mixture into the dry mixture and briefly blend with a whisk. Add water, as needed, to make a loose batter.

4. Fill the muffin tins 3/4 full with the batter. Bake until they are golden brown and a toothpick inserted in the middle comes out dry, 25 - 30 minutes.

5. Allow the muffins to cool for 10 minutes in the tins before removing to a wire rack.

variation

- Add 1/2 cup toasted sunflower seeds in step #3.

baked corn tortilla chips

6 - 8 servings

Although you can now buy baked tortilla chips at the store, there's nothing like making your own hot, fresh chips. They are surprisingly easy to make. Keep corn tortillas on-hand in the freezer so you can whip up a fresh batch any time. Serve them with Festive Tortilla Soup, *page 64, and your favorite salsa.*

ingredients

> 1 dozen corn tortillas

directions

1. Preheat the oven to 350°F.

2. Cut the tortillas into six pie-shaped wedges or strips. Arrange them on a cookie sheet and bake until they are so crispy, you can snap them in half, approximately 15 - 20 minutes. Check on them to prevent burning.

3. Refrigerate or freeze in glass jars.

cook's tip

- Use your favorite cookie cutter to make unique-shaped chips for children on special occasions.

sesame wheat crackers

60 1-inch square crackers

I made these crunchy golden crackers by the thousands in my Phoenix deli. Their crispness and addictive flavor will satisfy your craving for crunch. Once you've made them, you may never want store-bought crackers again.

wet ingredients

2/3 cups water

2 TBS. sesame oil

1/2 tsp. unrefined sea salt

dry ingredients

2 cups whole wheat bread flour

2 TBS. sesame seeds

directions

1. Preheat the oven to 400°F. Brush two cookie sheets with oil and set aside.

2. Combine the wet ingredients in a blender. Process until uniform in color.

3. Add the flour to a bowl. Pour the wet mixture into the flour and briefly blend with a whisk. Knead for 2 minutes. Cover with a damp cloth and refrigerate for about half an hour.

4. Pat the dough onto the cookie sheets and roll out very thin. Sprinkle sesame seeds on top. Use the rolling pin to press the seeds into the dough. Score for the desired cracker size by making shallow cuts into the dough before baking. This facilitates removing and breaking apart the finished crackers.

5. Bake until golden brown, 15 - 20 minutes. Break them along the score lines.

variation

• Add 1 clove of minced garlic to step #3.

cook's tips

• Crackers along the edges of the cookie sheet usually cook faster and need to be removed sooner than those in the center of the pan.
• Place a pan of cold water in the oven for even baking and to prevent burning.

homemade sesame-rice crackers

40 1-inch square crackers

Eat as many of these wheat-free, fat-free crackers as you want without feeling guilty.
Serve with Adzuki Chestnut Soup, *page 103, or* Double Chickpea Soup, *page 51.*

ingredients

    2 cups water
    1 cup brown rice
  1/2 tsp. unrefined sea salt
    3 TBS. unhulled sesame seeds

directions

1. Bring 2 cups of water to a boil in a pressure cooker. Add the washed rice and the salt.

2. Lock the lid in place. Bring up to full pressure over high heat. Place a flame tamer under the pressure cooker and reduce the heat. Maintain high pressure for 45 minutes.

3. Preheat the oven to 325°F. Brush two cookie sheets with oil and set aside.

4. Quick-release the pressure. Add the sesame seeds and mash vigorously with a potato masher.

5. When cool enough to handle, divide the sticky rice mixture into 2 balls. Press each ball into a firm, flat disc.

6. With damp hands, place a disc in the center of a cookie sheet and press into a flat rectangle. Cover with wax paper and roll out until as thin as possible. Remove the waxed paper and score into squares or rectangles. Repeat with the other disc.

7. Bake until crisp, 35 - 45 minutes. They will not brown.

variation

• Roll out between two sheets of parchment paper. Score with a pizza cutter. Set directly on the oven wire racks and bake until the top parchment paper falls off and the crackers are golden brown, about 40 minutes.

garlic toast

4 servings

Feel free to indulge in this low-fat version of garlic toast with any soup or pasta.

ingredients

- 1 garlic clove, minced
- 2 slices naturally leavened bread
- 2 tsp. extra-virgin olive oil

directions

1. Preheat the oven to 400°F.

2. **Meanwhile,** mash the garlic and oil together in a blender or a suribachi to form a paste.

3. Use a knife or cookie cutters to cut the bread into the desired shapes. Brush the garlic paste on 1 side of the bread. Place the bread cut-outs, oiled-side up, on a baking sheet.

4. Bake until golden, about 7 minutes.

notes

appendix

lorna's curry powder

3/4 cup

You will wonder how you ever used anything but this fragrant, flavorful, homemade curry powder. Lorna Sass recommends storing homemade curry powder in a glass jar in the refrigerator for up to three months.

ingredients

1/4 cup whole coriander seeds
2 TBS. whole cumin seeds
4 tsp. whole fennel seeds
2 tsp. white mustard seeds
1/2 tsp. white peppercorns
3 whole cloves

3 TBS. turmeric
4 tsp. ground ginger
1 tsp. ground cinnamon
1/4 tsp. ground nutmeg
1 pinch cayenne

directions

1. Preheat a large, nonstick skillet.

2. **Meanwhile**, combine the coriander, cumin, fennel seeds, mustard seeds, peppercorns and cloves in a small bowl. Add to the heated skillet. Stir constantly until the seeds darken slightly and become aromatic, 30-60 seconds. Immediately transfer back to the bowl to cool down.

3. Place in a spice mill and grind to a fine powder. Add the remaining spices and stir to mix.

4. Transfer to a glass jar when room temperature. Refrigerate until needed.

variation

• Substitute ground white pepper for the whole peppercorns.

untomato sauce

2 quarts

Tomatoes cause my arthritis to flare up, so I've been unable to eat tomato sauce for years. I created this delicious sauce as an alternative and actually like it better than the "real thing." Gary Miller, at www.cybermacro.com, also raves about the taste of this sauce!

ingredients

- 1/2 tsp. extra-virgin olive oil
- 2 jumbo onions, cut into large pieces
- 6 garlic cloves, peeled and cut in half
- 2 pounds carrots, in large pieces
- 2 small beets, peeled and quartered

- 2 bay leaves, in a tea ball
- 2 tsp. dried basil
- 1 1/4 tsp. dried oregano
- 1/8 tsp. dried thyme
- 3 TBS. barley miso, or more to taste
- 1/4 cup umeboshi paste

directions

1. Heat the oil in a large stock pot. Sauté the onions until translucent, about 5 minutes. Add the garlic and stir constantly for 1 minute.

2. Add the carrots, beets and bay leaves. Add water to 1 inch below the surface of the vegetables. In this case, less is more. Bring to a boil and simmer, covered, for 45 minutes.

3. Add the basil, oregano and thyme. Simmer for 15 minutes.

4. Remove the bay leaves. Remove and reserve most of the broth. Remove about half of the beets and set aside.

5. Transfer the vegetables, miso and umeboshi paste to a blender. Process, adding just enough broth to reach a tomato sauce consistency. Add the beets, one at a time, to simulate the color of tomato sauce.

variation

- If you are not concerned about nightshade vegetables, substitute organic tomato sauce for the *Untomato Sauce*.

cook's tips

- The bay leaves are placed in a mesh tea ball for easy removal before blending the sauce.
- Ground oregano creates a smoother sauce than the common variety.
- Use boiling water in step #2 to save time.
- Prepare *Untomato Sauce* ahead of time and refrigerate or freeze in canning jars. Use in spaghetti, pizza and soup.

glossary

The majority of these foods are available at natural food stores. If you cannot find something, check the mail-order list. The quality of ingredients is of paramount importance for the best taste.

Adzuki Bean, Azuki Bean [ad-zoo-kee, ah-zoo-kee] Adzuki beans are small, sweet, purple-colored beans, reputed to be diuretic and highly beneficial to the kidneys.

Agar, Agar-Agar [ah-gahr] This sea vegetable is also known as kanten. It contains a complex starch that acts as a gelling agent. Used in desserts, it is a healthful alternative to gelatin, which contains ground horse's hooves or other animal parts.

Amazake [a-mah-sah-kee] This fermented rice drink is sweet and dense in nutrients. It contains complex sugars, so it supplies the body with long-lasting energy. It has the consistency of a milk shake and is available in a variety of flavors, including almond, mocha java, vanilla bean, hazelnut and original. You can find it in the freezer or refrigerator section in natural food stores.

Arrowroot Powder This tropical root yields a white starch which is used to thicken sauces. Once thickened, the arrowroot mixture becomes clear. Be aware that over stirring can cause the sauce to become thin again. Arrowroot is high in calcium and is nutritionally superior to cornstarch. However, there is a third alternative that I prefer, kudzu. See Kudzu.

Baking Powder Baking powder is used as a leavening agent to make baked goods rise. Unfortunately, most commercial brands contain unhealthful aluminum compounds. Buy aluminum-free brands, such as Rumford.®

Balsamic Vinegar This Italian vinegar is aged in wooden barrels. It graces foods with its rich color and complex flavor, which is both sweet and sour.

Barley Malt Syrup This syrup is similar to molasses in taste and appearance. It is made by cooking sprouted barley until it becomes a sweet syrup. Its primary component is maltose, a complex sugar, which provides longer-lasting energy than sweeteners made of simple sugars.

Bragg® Liquid Aminos Made from soybeans, Bragg® Liquid Aminos is an unfermented alternative to tamari. It is not a personal favorite, but you may want to use it if you are avoiding fermented foods.

Brown Rice Syrup This thick, amber-colored syrup is commonly used to sweeten desserts. Traditional rice syrup is produced by combining whole, sprouted barley with cooked brown rice. In contrast, domestic brands use extracted barley enzymes instead of whole barley to produce the syrup. This affects the overall quality and taste. Meredith McCarty, author of *Sweet and Natural*, recommends Sweet Cloud® brown rice syrup because it is still made traditionally. Refrigerate rice syrup after opening.

Brown Rice Vinegar Imported from Japan, brown rice vinegar has a smooth, mild flavor. Buy brands that are traditionally brewed. This means that the vinegar has been fermented for approximately one year, assuring superior quality.

Bulgur Wheat, Bulgar, Bulghur Bulgur consists of wheat kernels that have been steamed, dried and crushed. It has a nutty flavor and cooks much faster than whole wheat kernels. Although available in coarse, medium and fine grinds, I usually choose the coarse variety for its chewy texture. Store in the refrigerator or freezer.

Burdock root Burdock, also known as gobo in Asian grocery stores, is a light brown root vegetable. It grows along the edge of the woods, identified by its huge, green leaves and burrs. It is also cultivated for its healing minerals and sweet, earthy flavor. It is reputed to be a blood purifier and to help curb the proverbial "sweet tooth."

Canola Oil Extracted from rape seed, canola oil is lower in saturated fats than any other oil. Because it has a neutral taste, it is a great choice for baking. Refrigerate after opening. See also Spectrum Naturals® Canola Spread.

Chestnuts Even though chestnuts are less than ten percent fat, they offer a rich, sweet taste. They are available fresh in the fall or dried and canned year round. Refrigerate dried chestnuts to keep grain moths at bay.

Chickpeas Chickpeas, also known as garbanzo beans, have a delicious, sweet flavor. While most other beans weigh in at 0.5% fat, chickpeas contain 2.6%. This makes them rich and creamy.

Chipotle Chile Peppers, Dried [chi-poe-tlay] Chipotles, smoked jalapeño peppers, are prized for their distinct blend of hot, smoky and sweet flavors.

Corn Grits and Cornmeal Both made from dried, ground corn, these foods are often confused with each other. Corn grits are coarse and are used to make cooked cereal and polenta. Cornmeal is finer and is used to make muffins and cornbread. Both must be kept refrigerated to prevent rancidity.

Corn Oil This oil has a buttery flavor, so I occasionally like to use it in baking. However, it is not as healthful as canola oil and tends to make baked goods heavy.

Couscous [koos-koos] This quick-cooking grain is made from steamed semolina wheat, which has been oven-dried. It is best stored in the refrigerator.

Currant A currant is a dried Zante grape. It resembles a tiny, dark raisin, but has a tangy edge. They are perfect for baking since they hold their shape better than raisins.

Daikon [dye-kon] Sweet and pungent, this long, white radish has great healing properties. According to traditional medicine, it aids in the digestion of fat and protein and is effective against many bacterial and fungal infections.

Dulse [duhlss] This tasty sea vegetable is particularly delicious cooked in oatmeal. Before cooking, remove the small shells that are often packaged with it.

EdenBlend® beverage My replacement for milk, EdenBlend® beverage is a combination of organic rice and soy beverages. I prefer it over rice milk or soy milk, since it has a lighter taste and complementary proteins.

EnerG® Egg Replacer EnerG® is a vegetarian and gluten-free egg substitute. For those avoiding nightshade vegetables, be aware that it contains potato starch. Alternatively, you can substitute an equal amount of arrowroot powder.

Florets This term refers to bite-sized pieces cut from the heads of broccoli or cauliflower.

Garlic This pungent food is famous for its healing powers. It is reputed to be antibacterial, anticarcinogenic and antifungal. It is also known to lower blood pressure and cholesterol. See *The Healing Power of Food* for a complete list of health benefits. To easily remove the papery skin, set the clove on a hard surface. Place the flat side of a chef's knife blade against the clove and lightly smash with the side of the fist. This will cause the skin to break away. Separate individual cloves and cut off the root end. To prevent wooden cutting boards from absorbing the strong flavors of garlic and onions, wet the board before cutting them. I mince garlic instead of pressing it, since this texture works better in most dishes. Sauté garlic for only one minute or it will become bitter. Store leftover cloves in a cool, dry place. If there is a green sprout in the center of the garlic clove, discard it. It is old and will taste bitter.

Gingerroot This pungent vegetable is superb in stir-fries and dressings. According to traditional medicine, it increases circulation, stimulates digestion and is an effective remedy for motion sickness. To effectively shred ginger, use a ginger grater. Oriental and natural food stores carry porcelain or aluminum ginger graters, although I prefer stainless steel. To make ginger juice, place grated pulp into the palm of the hand. Squeeze out the juice by making a tight fist. You might want to do this over a strainer so that no bits of pulp accidentally fall into the juice. Store fresh ginger in the refrigerator in a paper bag. Slice off the shredded edge when you are ready to use it again.

Gomashio [goh-mah-shee-o] This is a condiment made from toasted, crushed sesame seeds and unrefined sea salt. It is a perfect accompaniment to grains and other foods.

Hato Mugi Barley [hah-to moo-gee] See Job's Tears.

Herbamere® This organic herb seasoning can be used to make an instant vegetable stock to boost the flavor of soups. Use one half teaspoon per quart of water. Be aware that it contains salt, so adjust your own recipes accordingly.

Hot Sesame Oil This oil is extracted from toasted sesame seeds and red chili peppers. It imparts a fiery edge to stir-fries.

Job's Tears Job's tears, also known as hato mugi, is a pearl-shaped grain with a hearty, chewy texture. Traditional medicine believes that it helps reduce arthritis symptoms, urinary problems, cysts and tumors. Combine with other grains or add to soups. My favorite use for these little gems is in *Green Split Pea Soup*, page 42. Pick over for stones and bits of hulls. Soak at least an hour before cooking. See Mail Order Sources.

Kanten [kan-tehn] See Agar.

Kasha Kasha is toasted buckwheat. It is amber in color and has a wonderful, nutty flavor. Plain buckwheat tends to be bland unless you toast it yourself. Related to rhubarb, buckwheat is not a true grain, but it is cooked like one. Nor is it related to wheat. Buckwheat is gluten-free and, therefore, excellent for people with allergies. Its warming nature makes it popular in cold places like Siberia and Michigan! Buckwheat is rich in protein, iron and vitamins E and B complex. In addition, buckwheat has 100% more calcium than any grain and has all eight essential amino acids, rare in the true grain family. Kasha is best stored in the refrigerator.

Kombu [kohm-boo] This dried sea vegetable, also known as kelp, was the original MSG, acting as a natural flavor enhancer. When cooked with beans, it makes them easier to digest. Available at natural food stores.

Kudzu [kood-zoo] This root starch is used as a thickening agent in sauces and icings. First, dissolve it in cool water. Then, cook until thickened and translucent, about five minutes. According to traditional medicine, kudzu is beneficial to the intestines and stomach. It is also used to make blood more alkaline and to relieve acute muscle pain. Kudzu has more medicinal properties than arrowroot powder with twice the thickening power. One tablespoon of kudzu thickens one cup of liquid. See Arrowroot Powder.

Kukicha Twig Tea [ku-kee-cha] When organic, this low-caffeine tea is naturally sweet. High in minerals, it is made from the stems and twigs of tea bushes.

Kuzu See Kudzu.

Legumes This plant family includes beans, lentils, peanuts and peas. All grow in pods and are high in protein. They are generally referred to as beans.

Natural Hickory Seasoning Made by Wright's® Liquid Smoke®, this flavoring offers a wood-grilled taste to foods. It is made from water and a natural mesquite smoke concentrate.

Maple Syrup On average, 40 gallons of maple tree sap are required to produce one gallon of maple syrup. It is sold in various grades. AA grade is perfect for dressings and sauces. B grade is often used for baking. Keep in mind that maple syrup is made up of simple sugars, so it is not as healthful as brown rice syrup. Refrigerate after opening.

Millet This gluten-free grain has more iron than any other grain. It helps balance blood sugar levels and is one of the few grains which is alkaline. Japanese Kibi millet is so sweet and tasty that it is well worth the time and money to send for it. See Mail Order Sources.

Mirin [mihr-ihn] This heavenly cooking wine comes from Japan. It is made from sweet brown rice, koji and water. Its light, sweet taste balances the flavors of strong condiments like shoyu, miso and vinegar. Common commercial brands are almost always chemically brewed and sweetened with sugar. Buy only naturally brewed varieties, available at natural food stores.

Miso [mee-soh] Miso is an aged, fermented soybean paste made from soybeans, salt and usually a grain. The two main types of miso are dark and light. Dark commonly refers to barley miso, which has been aged for at least two years. It has a salty taste and is used in dark-colored soups, gravies and stews. Light miso has a sweeter taste because it contains less salt and is fermented for less time. It is used in light-colored soups and sauces. Regardless of the type, unpasteurized miso contains friendly bacteria, high quality protein and digestive enzymes. Since digestive enzymes are destroyed by high heat, do not boil after adding miso to the dish. Store miso in the refrigerator.

Mochi [moh-chee] Mochi is cooked, sweet brown rice that has been pounded and formed into flat cakes. It is a superb, wholesome snack or breakfast food, since it offers long-lasting energy. Traditionally, mochi is considered excellent for pregnant and lactating women. It is available in the freezer or refrigerator section in natural food stores.

Mustard, Prepared Natural This prepared condiment is made of dried mustard seeds mixed with vinegar and spices. Stoneground mustard has a lovely flavor and a rustic feel.

Napa Cabbage Also known as Chinese Cabbage, this delicate, light green vegetable resembles Romaine lettuce with its tight head, barrel shape. It has a lighter texture and cooks more quickly than regular green cabbage.

Nuts Store shelled nuts in the refrigerator or freezer, otherwise they will become rancid. To toast nuts, preheat a large, nonstick skillet. Rinse nuts through a strainer and pour into the hot skillet. Dry-roast until nuts are dry and light brown in color, about eight minutes. Stir continuously with a wood spoon or rice paddle to prevent burning.

Oat Flour Oat flour can be made fresh at home. Simply place rolled oats in a blender and blend until a flour-like consistency has been reached, about one minute.

Olive Oil This fruity oil is frequently used in salad dressings and pasta dishes. High in vitamin E, olive oil is one of the most stable vegetable oils. The term extra-virgin means that the oil comes from the first stage of mechanically-pressed olives. This is in contrast to later extractions when chemicals and heat are used, destroying flavor and trace nutrients. Store in the refrigerator to preserve flavor and freshness.

Olives Olives are either green or black. The green ones are simply unripened black olives. Regardless of the type, the tastiest olives are those that have been naturally cured in a salt solution. My favorite olive, Kalamata, can be found in most ethnic markets and natural food stores.

Oregano I prefer dried, ground oregano which imparts a smooth consistency to any dish, unlike the common leaf variety.

Pasta While whole wheat pasta may be the healthiest choice, it is too heavy for most people to truly enjoy. I prefer wholesome noodles made from lighter, whole-grain flours, such as artichoke, corn, kamut, quinoa, rice and buckwheat. Each has a distinct color, flavor and shape. Semolina pasta, made from refined durum wheat, is the most popular variety. My favorite brand is the readily available DeCecco.®

Peanut Butter Commonly thought of as a nut, a peanut is actually a legume. Although high in oil, peanut butter is also high in protein with no cholesterol. While natural peanut butter contains only peanuts and salt, commercial brands contain sugar and many chemical additives for marketing appeal. A significant drawback to peanut butter is that a carcinogenic mold, aflatoxin, is commonly found on peanuts grown in damp conditions. Buy only brands which are certified to be free of aflatoxin, such as Arrowhead Mills.® Keep refrigerated.

Pepper Black pepper is considered an irritant to the intestines. I substitute its milder sister, white pepper, in dishes that call for pepper.

Polenta Polenta is the Italian name for traditional porridge made from cornmeal. For a speedy version made in the pressure cooker, see page 108, in *Lenore's Natural Cuisine*.

Pumpkin Seeds Pumpkin seeds are not from a pumpkin, but rather from a South American squash. They are not only a good source of Omega-3 fatty acids, zinc, iron and calcium, but contain 29% protein. They are most delicious when dry-roasted. See Nuts for dry-roasting instructions.

Quinoa [keen-wah] Quinoa is grown in the high valleys of the Andes. It was the staple food for the Incas because it thrives under the most rugged conditions. Quinoa, like amaranth, is a member of the goosefoot family, rather than being a true grain. It is easy to digest, quick-cooking and acts as a high-energy endurance food. As an added bonus, it has the highest protein content of any grain. It contains all eight essential amino acids, including lysine, which is rarely found in the plant kingdom. Rinse thoroughly before cooking to remove the bitter saponin coating.

Radicchio [rah-dee-kee-oh] This is the Italian name for red chicory. It is a mildly bitter, bright purple vegetable that looks like a miniature red cabbage. Radicchio is often used to perk up the flavor and color of leafy green salads.

Rice, Brown Brown rice is a whole grain, with only the inedible, outer husk removed. It is a good source of B vitamins, minerals, carbohydrates and fiber. In cool weather, I pressure-cook short-grain rice. In warmer weather, I like to boil brown basmati, the most aromatic long-grain variety.

Rice Milk Just as you would imagine, rice milk is a beverage made from rice. Check the package label for ingredients, as all rice milks are not made from whole brown rice. See EdenBlend® beverage.

Rice, Sweet Brown Sweet brown rice is more glutinous, higher in protein and sweeter than regular brown rice. It is traditionally made into mochi. You can cook it with other grains for a sweet change.

Rolled Oats These are whole oat groats that have been flattened between two rollers to shorten cooking time. See also Oat Flour.

Roma® This instant grain cereal beverage is made from chicory and roasted malt barley. It is caffeine-free and has a robust, full-bodied taste. With only ten calories per teaspoon, Roma® is an excellent coffee substitute. Other brands of instant grain cereal beverages are Bamboo,® Cafix,® Pero® and Sip.®

Rutabaga [roo-tah-bay-gah] Surprisingly, this vegetable is a cross between turnip and wild cabbage. It is large and round with a light yellow and purple skin. It tastes slightly sweet and is high in fiber. Supermarket rutabagas are almost always waxed, so peel off the skin.

Sauerkraut Sauerkraut, a naturally-fermented condiment, is made from cabbage and salt. It contains friendly bacteria which aid digestion. Buy only the refrigerated, unpasteurized variety. All other sauerkraut is pasteurized, which destroys its friendly bacteria and zingy flavor.

Scallions Scallions, also known as green onions or spring onions, conveniently keep for several weeks in the refrigerator. Keep them on hand for a fresh, green garnish for soups and pasta.

Sea Salt Unrefined sea salt is pure sea salt that has been hand-harvested and air-dried. It contains all the trace elements found in sea water with no chemical additives. The best natural sea salt brands are Muramoto,® Lima,® Celtic® and Si.®

Sea Vegetables Also known as sea weed, sea vegetables are the most plentiful food on earth. They draw bountiful trace minerals, essential for the body's health, from the sea brine in which they grow. For example, two tablespoons of sea vegetables contain two to ten times more calcium than a cup of milk. Sea vegetables also boast an astounding 30% protein. In addition, researchers report that sea vegetables help reduce blood cholesterol, prevent thyroid deficiencies and remove metallic and radioactive elements from the body. Dried sea vegetables do not require refrigeration.

Sesame Oil This light, nutty-flavored oil can be used in every cooking style.

Sesame Seeds Sesame seeds have a slightly sweet, nutty flavor. They are remarkably high in calcium and they contain more iron than liver and more protein than nuts. Unhulled sesame seeds offer more nutrients than the hulled variety. Black sesame seeds can be an attractive garnish, but only purchase them from a reputable natural food store. Oriental stores typically sell imitation black seeds that have been dyed. Store sesame seeds in the refrigerator or freezer.

Shiitake Mushrooms [shee-tah-kay] According to traditional medicine, dried shiitake mushrooms help dissolve fat, cysts and cholesterol, and act as a blood cleanser. They are also delicious. To prepare, soak dried mushrooms for several hours before cooking. They can be left to soak for up to eight hours. Or, pour boiling water over them and soak for fifteen minutes. Trim off and discard stems.

Shoyu [shoh-you] Shoyu is the Japanese name for naturally-fermented soy sauce. Made from soybeans, roasted wheat and salt, it is fermented in wooden kegs for at least eighteen months. While shoyu does not require refrigeration, a lacy, white mold may appear on the surface of the liquid. It is a harmless fermenting agent. Skim it off and simmer the shoyu for five minutes. To prevent it from returning, refrigerate. See Tamari and Soy Sauce.

Soba [soh-buh] Soba refers to Japanese noodles made from 100% buckwheat flour or a combination of buckwheat and another flour.

Soy Milk Soy milk is a beverage with as much protein as whole cow's milk, but one-tenth the chemical residues, one-third the fat, fewer calories and no cholesterol. Moreover, it is packed with essential B vitamins and has about ten times more iron than its dairy counterpart. A drawback is that it is darker in color than cow's milk. I recommend EdenBlend® beverage, a soy-rice blend, instead. I also suggest that it be mixed with cow's milk during a transition to a non-dairy diet.

Soy Sauce Soy sauce is a generic term for a dark, salty sauce made by fermenting boiled soybeans with roasted wheat or barley and salt. When traditionally made, a long aging process imparts a rich, complex flavor. Commercial soy sauce, on the other hand, is quickly made and chemically modified. It contains corn syrup and artificial flavors and colors. Soy sauce does not require refrigeration. See Tamari and Shoyu.

Spectrum Naturals® Canola Spread This non-hydrogenated, non-dairy spread is made with pure canola oil. It has a buttery taste without the cholesterol. This is the spread I recommend to my students as a healthful alternative to butter or margarine.

Squash There are two major categories of squash: summer and winter. The most popular summer varieties are zucchini and yellow squash. Winter squash are my favorite, because they are so sweet. They include buttercup, kabocha, butternut, sweet dumpling and delicata. Less sweet are acorn and spaghetti squash. No matter what the variety, the more dense the squash, the sweeter it is.

Sweet Potatoes Sweet potatoes are not related to white potatoes or yams. True yams are tubers of a tropical climbing plant. In spite of this, dark sweet potatoes are often referred to as yams. While sweet potatoes come in several varieties, "garnet yams" are my favorite. They have dark red skins and are intensely sweet, almost like candy.

Tahini [tah-hee-nee] Tahini is made of ground, hulled sesame seeds. It is sometimes referred to in recipes as sesame tahini. It has a nutty flavor and is high in calcium. Be careful when choosing a brand. Canned tahini is often bitter, grainy and thick. I prefer Arrowhead Mills® raw, organic tahini, which has a creamy texture and a delicate flavor.

Tamari [tuh-mah-ree] Traditionally, tamari was the liquid by-product of miso production. Today, it refers to a wheat-free soy sauce made with traditional processing methods. I prefer the full-bodied flavor of shoyu, although tamari is a good choice for people with wheat allergies. Tamari does not require refrigeration.

Tea Popular black tea, such as orange pekoe, is made from the leaves of the tea-shrub. Black tea contains, on average, half as much caffeine as coffee. Green tea, although reputed to be healthful, contains the same amount of caffeine as black tea. A better choice is herbal tea, which is made of an infusion of herbs, flowers and spices. Celestial Seasonings® offers innumerable choices. Also, try kukicha twig tea and caffeine-free teas like Good Earth® Original Sweet and Spicy Herb Tea and Traditional Medicinals® Ginger Aid® Tea. See Kukicha Twig Tea.

Teff Teff is a minuscule cereal grain. A staple in Ethiopia, it has a mildly sweet and nutty flavor. Teff is a good source of complex carbohydrates, but is higher in protein and calcium than most other grains.

Tempeh [tehm-pay] Tempeh is a fermented soybean product originating from Indonesia. It boasts 50% more protein than hamburger and is cholesterol-free. It has a hearty texture and is an excellent source of energy. Its distinct flavor is complemented by strong seasonings such as ginger, garlic, vinegar and mustard. Try steaming, grilling or sautéing it in a few drops of oil. Tempeh is available in the freezer or refrigerator section in natural food stores.

Toasted Sesame Oil This rich, dark oil is extracted from toasted sesame seeds. Its divine fragrance and nutty flavor enhance stir-fries.

Tofu Made from soybeans, tofu is rich in calcium and is a cholesterol-free protein source. According to oriental medicine, tofu is reputed to have a cooling nature and is beneficial to people who have high blood pressure. Traditionally, cooling tofu was never an ingredient in cold desserts. People with a delicate digestive tract would be better off not eating sweet, oily desserts made with tofu. When prepared this way, it can cause digestive problems.

Tofu has a blandness which makes it a versatile ingredient, readily absorbing other flavors. It comes in smooth, white cakes in two basic varieties. Soft tofu has a higher water content than firm tofu and is used for making soups and creamy sauces. In contrast, firm tofu is used for stir-frying, baking and grilling. Compress firm tofu in a pickle press or between two cutting boards for twenty minutes to expel excess water. This process allows additional flavor to be absorbed by the tofu.

Both kinds of tofu are usually found refrigerated in the produce department or dairy case at grocery stores and always at natural food stores. I prefer refrigerated tofu over the variety that is packaged in an aseptic box. To store leftover tofu, leave it in the container covered with fresh water. If the water is changed every other day, the tofu will keep for one week. When it starts to turn pink and smells rotten, it is rotten, so throw it away!

Udon [ew-dohn] These thick, Japanese wheat noodles look like fettuccini. Since they are made by traditional methods, they are of high quality. My favorite variety, brown rice udon, contains 30% brown rice flour.

Umeboshi Paste [ew-meh-boh-shee] Umeboshi paste is made from puréed umeboshi plums. It adds a salty, sour taste to salad dressings and sauces. It is wonderful lightly spread inside of nori rolls and on corn on the cob.

Umeboshi Plums These bright pink plums have a salty, sour flavor. They are considered a natural antibiotic and are exceptionally high in iron. Umeboshi plums are made from unripe plums, salt and shiso leaves. They are fermented in a wooden keg for one year. Refrigeration is not required. See also Umeboshi Vinegar and Paste.

Umeboshi Vinegar Umeboshi vinegar is a by-product of umeboshi plum production. This salty, sour condiment is delicious sprinkled on salad and steamed greens.

Vanilla Vanilla, an aromatic bean pod of the orchid, is processed in a number of ways for use as a flavoring. Vanilla extract contains 35% alcohol. Vanilla flavor, on the other hand, is made with a glycerin base rather than alcohol. Purchase only natural vanilla flavor or extract as others are of questionable quality. Artificial vanilla is made from sugar, alcohol, artificial color and vanillin, a by-product of paper making. I use my old bottle of artificial vanilla to keep the refrigerator smelling heavenly. Pour a small amount of artificial vanilla on a damp dishcloth and wipe inside refrigerator walls.

Vinegar, Natural Natural vinegar refers to a delightfully salty, sour condiment which is naturally fermented for about a year. This is in sharp contrast to commercial vinegar, which is chemically fermented overnight. See Balsamic Vinegar, Brown Rice Vinegar and Umeboshi Vinegar.

Wakame [wah-kah-meh] Wakame is a dried, quick-cooking sea vegetable, most often used in miso soup. See Sea Vegetables.

Wheat Berry A whole wheat berry is the unprocessed wheat kernel with all its nutrients intact.

Whole Wheat Pastry Flour Whole wheat pastry flour is made from finely ground, soft, spring wheat berries. Since it has a lower gluten content than bread flour, it produces lighter baked products.

Wild Rice Wild rice, with its impressive nutty flavor and chewy texture, is not from the rice family. Rather, it is a long-grain marsh grass, native to the Great Lakes area. It has more protein, minerals and B vitamins than barley, oats or wheat.

Zest Also known as peel, zest is the colored, outer-layer of skin on citrus fruit. Be careful not to grate the white underskin as it is bitter. It is best to use organic whenever possible to avoid wax, dyes and pesticides.

cutting methods

florets and matchsticks

shredded

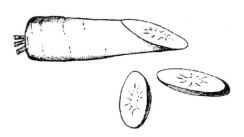

diagonal cut

half-rounds and matchsticks

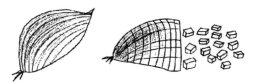

diced

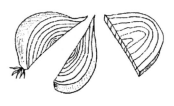

half-rounds

bean cooking chart

bean (1 cup dry)*	boiling		pressure-cooking		
	water (cups)	cooking time (minutes)	water (cups)	cooking time (minutes)	yield (cups)
adzuki	to cover	60	3	6	3
black (turtle)	4	90	3	11	2
black-eyed peas	3	40-60	3	3	2 1/4
chickpeas (garbanzos)	4	180	3	25	2 1/2
kidney	3	90	3	10-12	2
lentils (green, brown)	3	60-120	3	10	2
lentils (red)	3	45	3	5	2
pinto, anasazi	3	180	3	5	2
soybeans (black)	3	180+	3	25	2 1/2
split peas (yellow, green)	3	90	3	20	2
white (navy, great northern, lima)	3 1/2	120	3	7	2 1/4

* Soak 8 hours before cooking. For complete cooking instructions, see pp. 15-17, 79-106

food equivalents

Food	Amount	Equivalent Measure
broccoli stalk	1 large, 12 ounces	3 cups florets
cabbage	1 pound, 8 ounces	4 cups shredded
carrot	1 medium	1/2 cup sliced
cauliflower	1 medium	2 1/2 cups florets
celery	1 large stalk	2/3 cup sliced
corn, fresh	1 corn-on-the cob	1/2 cup
corn, frozen	20 ounces	4 cups
garlic	1 medium	1 tsp. minced or 1/2 tsp. dried
ginger	1 TBS. grated	1 tsp. juice
green beans	4 ounces	1 cup
herbs	1/3 tsp. dried	1 TBS. fresh
kudzu	1 tsp.	2 tsp. cornstarch or arrowroot
mirin	1 tsp.	1 tsp. sherry
mushrooms, fresh	8 ounces	1 1/2 cups sliced
onion	1 medium, 8 ounces	1 1/2 cups diced
onion	1 large, 12 ounces	2 cups diced
onion	1/2 tsp. dried	1 tsp. fresh
sea salt	1 tsp.	2 TBS. miso or shoyu
scallion	1 stalk	1/4 cup sliced
squash, winter	1 pound	3 cups diced
squash, summer	10 ounces	2 cups diced
yam or sweet potato	1 medium, 5 ounces	3/4 cup diced

recommended reading

Colbin, Annemarie. *Food and Healing*. New York: Ballantine, 1986.

Dufty, William. *Sugar Blues*. New York: Warner Books, 1975.

Ferré, Carl. *Pocket Guide to Macrobiotics*. Freedom, CA: The Crossing Press, 1997.

McDougall, M.D., John. *McDougall's Medicine-A Challenging Second Opinion*. Clinton, NJ: New Win Publishing, Inc., 1986.

Oski, M.D., Frank. *Don't Drink Your Milk!* Brushton, NY: Teach Services, 1996.

Pitchford, Paul. *Healing with Whole Foods*. Berkeley, CA: North Atlantic Books, 1993.

Robbins, John. *Diet for a New America*. Tiburon, CA: H. J. Kramer, 1998.

Robbins, John. *The Food Revolution*. Berkeley, CA: Publisher's Group West, 2001.

Varona, Verne. *Nature's Cancer-Fighting Foods*. New Jersey: Reward Books, 2001.

Wood, Rebecca. *The Whole Foods Encyclopedia (new and revised)*. New York: Penguin, 1999.

recommended web sites

Although the world wide web is so prolific and dynamic, here are some sites that people who are vegan or macrobiotic might find particularly useful. Most have links to other sites.

www.cybermacro.com

www.healingcuisine.com

www.lenoresnatural.com

www.macroamerica.com

www.macrobiotics.org

recommended cookbooks

Albert, Rachel. *Cooking with Rachel*. Oroville, CA: George Ohsawa Macrobiotic Foundation, 1989.

Baum, Lenore Yalisove, M.A. *Lenore's Natural Cuisine, Your Essential Guide to Wholesome, Vegetarian Cooking*. Farmington, MI: Culinary Publications, 2000.

Colbin, Annemarie. *The Natural Gourmet*. New York: Ballantine Books, 1989.

Estella, Mary. *Natural Foods Cookbook*. New York: Japan Publications, 1988.

Kushi, Aveline and Esko, Wendy. *Changing Seasons Cookbook*. Garden City Park, NY: Avery Publishing Group, 1985.

McCarty, Meredith. *American Macrobiotic Cuisine*. New York: St. Martin's Press, 1986.

McCarty, Meredith. *Fresh from a Vegetarian Kitchen*. New York: St. Martin's Press, 1989.

McCarty, Meredith. *Sweet & Natural*. New York: St. Martin's Press, 1999.

Lawson, Margaret. *The Naturally Healthy Gourmet*. Oroville, CA: George Ohsawa Macrobiotic Foundation, 1994.

Madison, Deborah. *Vegetarian Cooking for Everyone*. New York: Broadway Books, 1997.

Sass, Lorna J. *Lorna Sass's Complete Vegetarian Kitchen*. New York: Hearst Books, 1992.

Sass, Lorna J. *Great Vegetarian Cooking Under Pressure*. New York: William Morrow and Company, 1994.

Sass, Lorna J. *Short-Cut Vegetarian Cooking*. New York: Quill, 1997.

Sass, Lorna J. *The New Soy Cookbook*. San Francisco, CA: Chronicle Books, 1998.

Solomon, Jay. *Lean Bean Cuisine*. CA: PrimaPublishing, 1995.

Solomon, Jay. *Vegetarian Soup Cuisine*. CA: PrimaPublishing, 1996.

Turner, Kristina. *The Self-Healing Cookbook*. Grass Valley, CA: Earthtones Press, 1987.

Woodward, Jeff. *The Healing Power of Food*. MN: Traditional Cooking Arts, 1988.

mail order sources

natural foods and supplies

Gold Mine Natural Food Company
3419 Hancock Street
San Diego, CA 92110
(800) 862-2347

Kushi Institute Store
P.O. Box 7
Becket, MA 01223
(800) 645-8744

Lenore's Natural Cuisine
www.lenoresnatural.com
cookbooks, knives, Dutch ovens, miso strainers, nonstick skillets, pressure cookers, water purifiers and woks.

organic produce and prepared food

Diamond Organics
P.O. Box 2159
Freedom, CA 95019
(800) 922-2396

South River Miso
South River Farm
888 Shelburne Falls Road
Conway, MA 01341
(413) 369-4057

Whole Foods Market
www.wholefoodsmarket.com

index

Transform Your Health with Tantalizing Vegetarian Meals

Obesity and obesity-related diseases have become a national health challenge. While most of us want to eat healthier, it is difficult to translate the recommended guidelines into enticing, wholesome meals. Lenore Baum's innovative cookbook, *Lenore's Natural Cuisine, your essential guide to wholesome, vegetarian cooking,* addresses this need.

Baum's engaging, straightforward style informs, but does not overwhelm. She provides step-by-step instruction for over 100 scrumptious recipes with less than 15% fat and no dairy products or refined sugar. They will help you lose weight, increase your energy and feel satisfied!

More than 260 cook's tips transform this book from a collection of recipes into a mini-cooking course. These techniques will allow you to easily navigate your way through the exciting world of healthy, vegetarian cooking.

This easy-to-use book includes:

- Last-minute meals
- Delectable, guilt-free desserts
- Ways to conquer cravings
- Realistic menu planning
- Recipes that delight both adults and children
- Detailed dining out and travel-food suggestions
- Illustrations of cook's tools
- Otabind® lay-flat binding
- 256 pages, 7" x 10"

"Bravo for creating such an easy-reading guide to cooking balanced, vegetarian meals! It's chock-full of the kind of valuable tips and simple, appealing recipes that both seasoned and beginning cooks appreciate."
-Kristina Turner, author of *The Self-Healing Cookbook*

"Lenore's Natural Cuisine definitely delivers an essential guide to wholesome, vegetarian cooking. It is a great beginning for those of us who want the benefits of a plant-based diet, but who need inspiration and guidance to make it work... I'm off to make some of her Fabulous Brownies."
-Meredith McCarty, author of *Sweet and Natural, More Than 120 Sugar-Free and Dairy-Free Desserts*

**Lenore's Natural Cuisine
Your Essential Guide to
Wholesome, Vegetarian Cooking**

available for $23.95 (includes postage & tax):
www.lenoresnatural.com